PAN AMERICAN CLIPPER PLANES 1935 to 1945
WINGS TO THE ORIENT
A Pictorial History by Stan Cohen

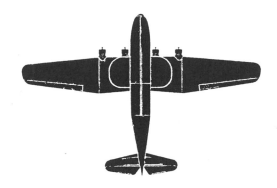

The *China Clipper,* with a Douglas Dolphin alongside, over downtown Honolulu, 1930s. courtesy Fred Nott

PAN AMERICAN CLIPPER PLANES 1935 to 1945
WINGS TO THE ORIENT
A Pictorial History by Stan Cohen

PICTORIAL HISTORIES PUBLISHING COMPANY
MISSOULA, MONTANA

LIBRARY OF CONGRESS
CATALOG CARD NUMBER 85-60319

ISBN 0-933126-61-1

First Printing: June 1985
Second Printing: February 1986
Third Printing: January 1987
Fourth Printing: January 1988
Fifth Printing: January 1990
Sixth Printing: February 1992
Seventh Printing: February 1994
Eighth Printing: April 1996

Typography: Arrow Graphics
Front Cover Art: Monte Dolack
Missoula, Montana

Printed in Canada
D.W. Friesen
Altona, Manitoba

PICTORIAL HISTORIES PUBLISHING COMPANY
713 South Third West
Missoula, Montana 59801

FOREWORD

I have seen and read hundreds of aviation books, including scores of what can—to use a simple description—be described as picture books. Many of the latter are best forgotten; they are too often quick collections of photographs of dubious quality, randomly obtained, casually presented, with—if the reader is lucky—a text full of inaccuracies. Occasionally, however, a picture book comes along which is in a quite different class. *Wings to the Orient* is a photographic delight, telling the whole story of Pan American Airways' Clipper Ships with a carefully assembled collection of photographs, supported by well-researched text. It has been put together with loving care, and if a good picture is worth, as the saying goes, a thousand words, then this book, in terms of quantity and quality of the photographs alone, is worth a million.

Stan Cohen begins, quite rightly, at the beginning, reviewing the forerunners of the great trans-ocean Martins and Boeings. He identifies the Sikorsky S-40 twin-boom flying boat as the very first Clipper, a name, incidentally, legally protected by Pan American for its exclusive use. Then came the great Sikorsky S-42s, which paved the way for trans-oceanic flying. While the Martin 130 opened service across the Pacific and the Boeing 314 across the Atlantic, we should never forget Igor Sikorsky's 1934 product which was several years ahead of its time, established completely new standards of long distance flying, and ushered in a new era.

The selection of photographs and drawings of the S-42 is excellent, but only a harbinger of better things to come. As the pages unfold, the reader is introduced not only to the elegance of the Martin M-130 as a flying machine, but is able also to savor the long 8000-mile trans-Pacific flight as it was flown, at a modest 140 mph or so. The Boeing 314's construction is the subject of a comprehensive photographic essay, appropriate to what most aviation scholars judge to have been the finest flying boat ever built. Other photographs and diagrams remind us that the Boeing giant required a crew of six to fly it, with the navigator's table alone taking up almost as much space as a 747 flight deck. There is an interesting shot of a Boeing 314 *model* production line. Only twelve Boeing 314s were built, so that the company probably built more models than actual examples of the 70-passenger flying boats.

The author does not neglect that all-important side of an airline operation—the ground operations. He provides generous coverage of the bases which Pan American had to build for the trans-Pacific route: rare shots of the San Francisco terminal at Treasure Island, nostalgic views of Pearl City, Hawaii; the visionary *North Haven* expedition to provide safe harbors at Wake and Midway islands; the dramatic scenes at Manila when the first scheduled flight arrived; and Hong Kong and Macao are not forgotten.

The people who made this great enterprise are also remembered. The parts played by the leading actors in the production: Juan Trippe, man of vision and determination; Ed Musick, the airline pilot's pilot: Hugo Leuteritz, pioneer of radio communications; and members of the pioneering crews: all are given due credit here. There is also a revealing photograph of the first passengers, whose identities reveal that to fly the Clippers was the privilege of the very rich.

Stan Cohen finds room for a special section for the philatelists, a few nostalgic shots for the movie buffs, and appendices showing the itineraries, schedules, and crew rosters of all the survey flights and the trans-Pacific inaugural, and Pan American's developing Clipper network until the outbreak of World War II. I would have liked to see an index, but the book is laid out so logically that this is almost superfluous.

We should be reminded that this great Pan American flying boat era was accomplished by only 28 aircraft: three Sikorsky S-40s, ten S-42s, three Martin M-130s, and twelve Boeing 314s. And the Boeings were used mainly on the Atlantic.

Wings to the Orient is for the discerning connoisseur who seeks a succinct account of the Clippers, the whole Clippers, and nothing but the Clippers. For the 95 percent of the readership who were not even born when these events took place, this is an important segment of the story of our national aviation heritage, evocative of a romantic and adventurous past. For the five percent who were around during the mid-1930s, I can guarantee a vicarious encounter which will reveal aspects of a unique experience which has been long forgotten, and, until Stan Cohen undertook this labour of love, hitherto unrevealed.

R.E.G. DAVIES
Curator of Air Transport
National Air and Space Museum
Washington, D.C.

INTRODUCTION

This book is about three types of airplanes, several individuals, and a new concept in overseas travel. The airplanes commonly called "Clippers," are the Sikorsky S-42, the Martin M-130, and the Boeing B-314. The individuals include Juan Trippe, founder of America's pioneering overseas airline, Pan Am. The new concept, formulated by Pan Am during the Depression days of the 1930s, involved island-hopping by air. The ocean to conquer was the vast Pacific.

Wings to the Orient is the first attempt to portray this massive undertaking through the use of historical photographs, some of which have never been published. It is fitting to bring out this book in 1985, for April 1985 is the 50th anniversary of Pan Am's first survey flight over the Pacific, and November marks the 50th anniversary of the first airmail flight from San Francisco to Manila.

Today, it is difficult to appreciate the significance of these first trans-Pacific flights. In modern jet aircraft, one can fly the same route—San Francisco to Manila—in just under a day's time. Yet in the early 1930s, the quickest way to the Orient was to spend three weeks on an ocean steamer. The Pan Am Clippers, which stopped overnight along the route, reduced that to a mere six days, a feat considered remarkable at the time.

The Clipper planes will always be fondly remembered. Despite the hardships of the Depression, the 1930s were a time of luxurious travel—luxury cruise ships plied the oceans, luxury trains criss-crossed the continents, and manufacturers were building a wide assortment of luxury automobiles. The Clippers were no exception—with comfortable berths, hot and cold running water, and meals served on linen-draped tables, they were the most luxurious planes ever to fly. Flying one for nearly a week to the Orient promised romance and adventure as well as good living.

This new trans-Pacific service lasted only five years—the first passenger flight took place in October 1936 and passenger service ended with America's entry into World War II immediately after the Pearl Harbor attack on Dec. 7, 1941. Yet in that short time, Pan American and her Clipper fleet made an invaluable contribution to aviation progress; the Clippers then helped out with the American war effort.

The story of Juan Trippe and his conquest of the Pacific is a tale of excitement, intrigue and daring, not to mention possible Japanese sabotage and enough adventures to fill several novels. As a pictorial history, *Wings to the Orient* can only touch on some of these aspects. For a detailed account of Pan American and Clipper history, one should read Robert Daley's *An American Saga: Juan Trippe and His Pan Am Empire.*

The days of the Clippers are gone forever, the service replaced decades ago by long-range jets. Even the planes are gone—not a single Clipper has been preserved by aviation museums. Through the use of historical photographs, however, *Wings to the Orient* attempts to bring to life trans-Pacific travel by Clipper during the halcyon days of the late 1930s. As you read this book, imagine yourself sitting in one of the Clipper's soft, luxurious chairs, the stewards bustling about around you, the huge expanse of the Pacific bright blue below you, the droning engines pulling you steadily toward the Orient.   —Stan Cohen

INTRODUCTION TO SECOND PRINTING

I was fortunate enough to be invited along on Pan Am's 50th Anniversary flight from San Francisco to Manila, Nov. 22-23, 1985. On this flight I got to meet some of the men who pioneered this route 50 years ago. Not only flight crewmen but people who were responsible for establishing the string of bases across the Pacific.

From these people and other contacts I discovered new information and photographs, both of which are incorporated in this second edition.

The wonderful trip I took made me appreciate the exciting adventure people must have experienced flying these magnificent flying boats in the 1930s.

Individuals who helped on the second edition include Alan Wright, son of flight crewman C.A. Wright; Jim Arey of Pan Am's Public Relations staff; Richard Paul Smyers and many others who contacted me to offer suggestions and corrections; Gordon Werne, who provided me with a piece of the *Philippine Clipper.*

ACKNOWLEDGMENTS

This book could not have been completed without the support and guidance of the public relations staff at Pan Am's New York headquarters. In particular, Ann Whyte and Dick Barkle were very helpful in the use of the company's extensive photo files and records and transportation to Hawaii, Manila, and Hong Kong for my research of the original Clipper stops.

The U.S. Air Force, Navy, and Coast Guard provided access to their military facilities on Wake and Midway islands. These islands usually are off-limits to civilians.

Several individuals provided photographs from their collections, including Stan Smith of Oakland, Calif.; Gordon Williams of Seattle, Wash.; Lt. Kevin House, U.S. Navy, Subic Bay, Philippines; Dr. Ron Thomas, Midway Island; and John L. Johnson, Jr., of Groton, Conn., who also provided access to his extensive collections regarding the postal history of the first flights. Additional photographs were obtained from the archives of the Navy and Marine Corps Museum at Treasure Island, San Francisco, Calif.; Hawaii State Archives, Honolulu, Hawaii; and the National Archives and Library of Congress, Washington, D.C.

Many photographs and information on the Clippers were obtained from Harvey Lippincott, United Technologies Archives, East Hartford, Conn., and Marilyn Phipps of Boeing Aircraft Archives, Seattle, Wash.

Others who provided help are Cindy Lilles, Manila Hotel, Manila; Ron Davies, curator of air transport at the National Air and Space Museum, Washington, D.C.; Enrique Santos, Philippines Air Lines; the staff of Pan Am's offices in Manila and Hong Kong; and the public affairs office of Naval Station Marianas, Guam, which also provided photos.

Monte Dolack, a nationally known poster artist who lives in Missoula, Mont., designed and produced the front cover art work. Peter Stark and Barry Kitterman of Missoula edited the manuscript, and Kitty Herrin of Arrow Graphics, Missoula, designed the typography.

My apologies to anyone inadvertently omitted. Any errors in this book are the responsibility of the author.

PHOTO SOURCES

SS—Stan Smith, Oakland, Calif.
GW—Gordon Williams, Seattle, Wash.
PAA—Pan American Archives, New York, N.Y.
LC—Library of Congress, Washington, D.C.
NA—National Archives, Washington, D.C.
B—Boeing Archives, Seattle, Wash.
UT—United Technologies Archives, East Hartford, Conn.
HA—Hawaii Archives, Honolulu, Hawaii
Recent photos were taken by the author or acknowledged to the source.

TABLE OF CONTENTS

The *Flying Cloud*, one of the great Clipper ships that plied the oceans of the world. The Pan American Clipper planes of the 1930s upheld the proud tradition of these ships. The word "Clipper" was made famous by a line of fast square-rigged sailing ships developed by Douglas McKay in the 1840s. Pan Am got the name copyrighted and used it on many of its planes even past the flying boat era.

National Maritime Museum, San Francisco

THE WORLD

MERCATOR PROJECTION

Capitals .... ⊕
International Boundaries .... — — —
Other Boundaries .... ·······
Ship Routes 631
NAUTICAL MILES

Copyright by C. S. HAMMOND & Co., N.Y.

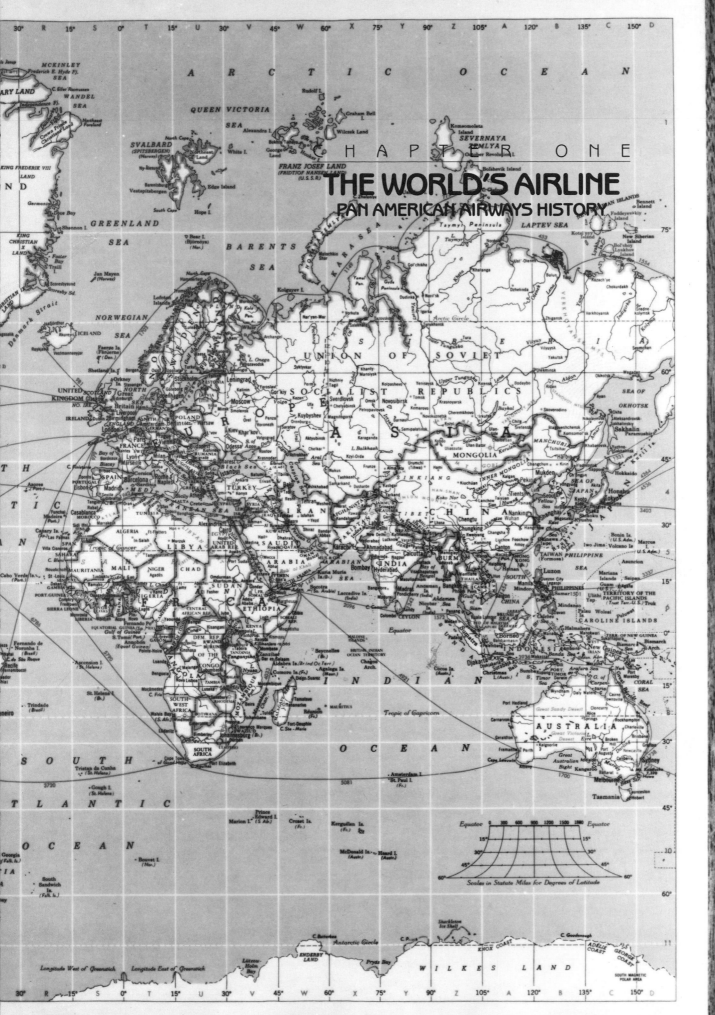

CHAPTER ONE

THE WORLD'S AIRLINE
PAN AMERICAN AIRWAYS HISTORY

Oct. 19, 1927, marked a milestone in the history of American commercial aviation. Although there were no cheering crowds to send off a single-engine, Fairchild FC-2 seaplane to Havana from Key West, this short flight saved Juan Trippe's fledgling airline.

In 1922, Trippe, who would later found the pioneering Pan American Airways, bought seven war-surplus, single-engine, pontoon biplanes (Model 49-B). With these planes he founded Long Island Airways, his first attempt in commercial aviation and his first chance to explore the air as a businessman instead of as a dare-devil stunt flyer. In the next few years Trippe operated several airlines and founded Eastern Air Transport.

In the early years of aviation, the key to establishing an airline with a regular flight schedule lay in obtaining an airmail contract from the government. Trippe merged his small airline, Eastern Air Transport, with the larger Colonial Airlines. The new company, renamed Colonial Air Transport, was awarded a contract for Air Mail Route No. 1, New York to Boston. With the contract in hand, Trippe proceeded to buy airplanes and set up business, overseeing the first airmail flight on July 1, 1926. The airline developed flights to Buffalo and a route was proposed to Chicago before an in-company squabble forced Trippe to leave Colonial.

He was not to be out of the aviation business for long. On June 2, 1927, Trippe and his college classmates, Sonny Whitney, William Vanderbilt, William Rockefeller and John Hambleton, incorporated a new airline company, the Aviation Corporation of America. Shortly thereafter, this new company merged with another fledgling airline, Pan American, and secured the mail contract for the route from Key West, Florida, to Havana, Cuba.

The contract stipulated that the first flight was to take place no later than October 19. A seemingly insurmountable problem arose, one that threatened to ground Trippe's airline. It was discovered that Pan Am's only plane, a Fokker F-7, would not be able to land at Key West's Meacham Field. The runway had not been completed. At the last minute, Trippe discovered that an FC-2 seaplane, being ferried to Haiti by Cy Caldwell, was in Key West for repairs. For a few hundred dollars, Caldwell was convinced to fly 30,000 letters to Havana, a distance of 90 miles. Several days later, regular scheduled service began between Florida and Cuba. Trippe's airline was off and running.

Trippe hired a Dutchman named Andre Priester to run his Key West operations. In order to keep the airline on a regular schedule, Priester set up rigid standards for both planes and pilots. He would be a mainstay throughout the formative years of the airline, serving Pan Am well into the 1950s.

Pan Am expanded its routes further and further south, first to Central America and later to South America. The airline dominated southern mail contract routes, buying up its main competition, the New York, Rio and Buenos Aires line (NYRBA). In 1929, Charles Lindbergh, the most well-known aviator of his day, joined Pan Am to develop new aircraft and to establish new routes, especially Asiatic and European routes. The world lay open to Juan Trippe and his new airline.

In 1931, Lindbergh and his wife Anne pioneered a route to China and Russia via Alaska. Pan Am quickly bought two small Alaska aviation companies, merging them into Pacific-Alaska Airways. Meanwhile, Pan Am's chief of communications, Hugo Leuteritz, had developed a new radio direction finder, making possible long-range navigation by air. Looking to Europe, Trippe sent the Lindberghs off to Greenland and Iceland in 1933 to explore a northern route to the continent.

Before U.S. entry into World War II involved Pan Am in wartime aviation, the airline had acquired either partial or complete ownership of airlines in Mexico, Guatemala, Colombia, Cuba, Brazil and China. With expansion into the Pacific, and its eyes on future Atlantic routes, Pan American was carrying the American flag throughout the world. The Pacific loomed as the biggest challenge, and the biggest gamble, the airline would face in the 1930s.

The *La Nina,* a single-engine Fairchild FC-2 seaplane that was chartered by Pan Am on Oct. 19, 1927, at Key West from West Indian Aerial Express. It carried the first mail from Key West to Havana thus preserving Pan Am's mail contract.   PAA

Pan Am's first airport was Meacham Field, Key West, Fla., in 1928. The plane is the airline's first aircraft, a Fokker F-7.

PAA

JUAN TRIPPE

The history of aviation has its share of famous individuals—Orville and Wilbur Wright, Glen Hammond Curtiss, Eddie Rickenbacker, Charles Lindbergh, Jimmy Doolittle, Amelia Earhart, however, from the field of commercial aviation, only a few names have earned a place in the memory of the general public. Perhaps this is understandable, as the break-throughs in commercial flying were often administrative in nature, less dynamic than spectacular first flights or heroic war records. Yet, any discussion of the individual men and women and their extraordinary contributions to the growth of aviation must include the name of Juan Trippe of Pan American Airways.

Born June 27, 1899, to a well-to-do family of English heritage, Trippe attended private schools in New York and Pennsylvania, as well as the Marconi Radio School and the Curtiss Flying School. Flying was to become his passion. He enrolled at Yale, but took a leave of absence in 1917 in order to join the navy and further his flight training. Although he saw no combat in World War I, the training he received in night flying and in the flying of bombers would prove invaluable in the years to come.

Following the war, Trippe returned to Yale, where he founded the Yale Flying Club. As he furthered his education, he shared his experience and enthusiasm for aviation with wartime friends such as William Vanderbilt and Cornelius Vanderbilt Whitney. It had long been assumed that, upon graduation, Trippe would follow his father's footsteps into the world of banking. But the lure of flying proved stronger than the force of tradition.

In 1922, Trippe founded his first airline business—Long Island Airways. From seven war-surplus, pontoon biplanes, purchased for $500 apiece, Trippe would build the aviation giant, Pan American World Airways. Beginning in the late 1920s, Trippe pioneered trans-ocean air service, opening new routes to South America, Europe and the Pacific. Trippe's airline developed new aircraft and innovations in flying procedures, airfield construction and communication and navigation techniques.

Trippe built Pan American into the world's dominant overseas carrier. His planes carried American prestige around the globe, as they returned with news of places that before had seemed little more than names in a geography text. With the outbreak of World War II, Trippe's planes flew troops and supplies around the world, making their contribution in every theater of war.

In 1928, Trippe married Betty Stettinius, the daughter of a wealthy Long Island family. The marriage would last through more than 40 years of Pan American growth, surviving the occasional gigantic losses and numerous corporate battles. In 1968, Trippe retired from the helm of the airline he had founded and piloted for 41 years. He died in April of 1981.

Juan Trippe as a naval aviator cadet, World War I.　　PAA

Juan Trippe, president and founder of Pan American World Airways, looking over his famous globe in 1942. By this time Pan Am was America's largest overseas carrier and was making tremendous contributions to the war effort.　　　PAA

Juan Trippe, Pan Am's visionary president.　　　PAA

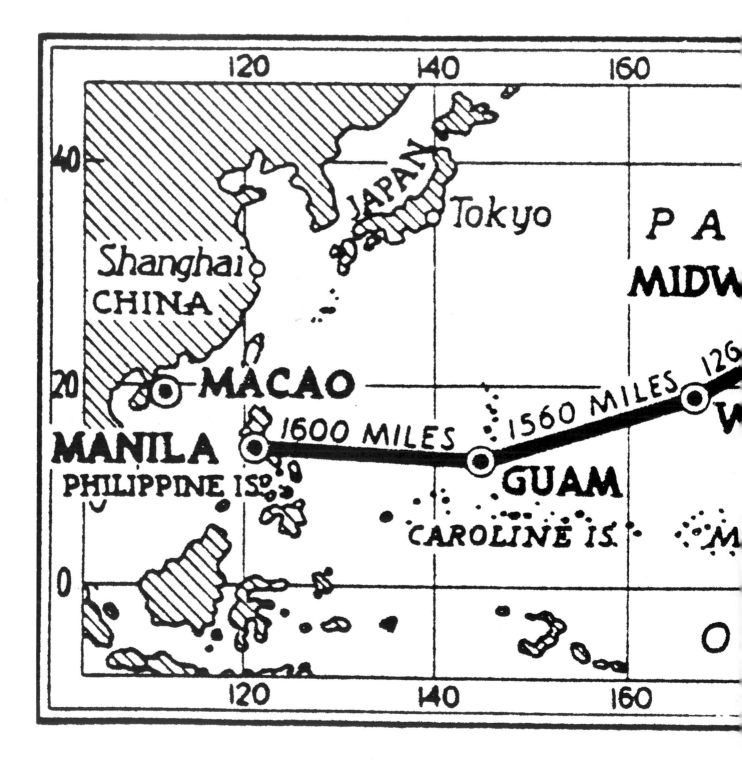

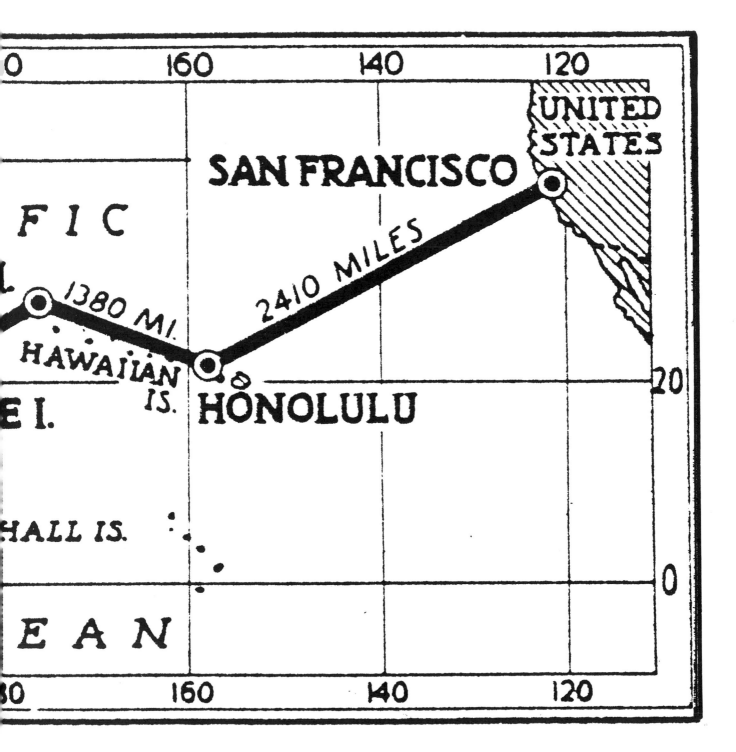

Crossing the Pacific Ocean would not be an easy task. In fact, the enormity of the Pacific would have prevented Trippe from attempting such a crossing had it not been for a succession of bad luck.

Trippe's venture in Alaska, where he had hoped to pioneer a route to China by way of Siberia, had been stymied by bad weather and U.S.-Russian political differences. His proposed routes to Europe were also falling victim to political intrigues, as well as to serious competition from European airlines.

In pioneering over-ocean flights to the Caribbean and South America, Trippe had invested heavily in the design and purchase of the S-42 and M-130 flying boats. Now he faced the necessity of finding a way for these planes to pay for themselves.

Facing obstacles to his European and Siberian routes, Trippe looked to the Pacific. He had the planes for a Pacific route. The M-130, designed for extended over-ocean trips, seemed ideally suited for a Pacific crossing. But once again, he would be pioneering flights where no one had flown before.

The Pacific route to China offered certain advantages over the northern route. A look at a map of the North Pacific shows a nearly straight line of stopping points on the way from California to Hong Kong. Hawaii, which was just within range of a cargo-laden M-130 taking off from California, had well-developed flying boat facilities. Midway had been home to a cable station since 1903, and featured a lagoon that could be made large enough to land clippers. At Guam, and in the Philippines, naval and flying-boat facilities had been established.

A major obstacle remained in the distance between Midway and Guam, over 2,600 miles. Searching for an intermediate point, Trippe consulted old logs of clipper ships at the New York Public Library, where he found references to Wake Island, a United States possession halfway between Midway and Guam. He could find no one who could say for sure how the island was governed. Water-landing possibilities, soil type, weather conditions, the availability of drinking water—all were a mystery.

Trippe sent his trusted associate, C.H. "Dutch" Schildhauer, to Washington, D.C., to do further research on these proposed Pacific lay-overs. From Washington, Schildhauer went on to Hawaii and Midway for on-site inspections. However, there was no ship to Wake, and no guarantee that the island could be made into a suitable base. With precious little information, Trippe gambled that a small island he had never seen would enable him to establish regular trans-Pacific flights.

A new route to China would only be practical if it could somehow be made profitable. Trippe contacted the U.S. Post Office Department. Postmaster General James Farley assured the Pan Am chief that the U.S. government was quite interested in Trippe's plan to conquer the Pacific skies. A Pacific route would connect important American outposts and show the American flag in China. The government of Japan had come to consider the Pacific Ocean as a Japanese domain. If American interests could be advanced through a private company, rather than through the threat of military force, so much the better. Trippe could count on being awarded a valuable airmail contract.

The stage was set for Pan Am's largest, most expensive, and with luck, most profitable expansion to date.

CHINA NATIONAL AVIATION CORPORATION (CNAC)

Juan Trippe had long planned to establish the eastern terminus of his trans-Pacific route on mainland China, preferably at Shanghai. He was to be prevented from doing so by an international agreement stipulating that all of the western nations and Japan would be allowed landing rights within China should any one of them be allowed to establish a base. China was not willing to grant such rights to the Japanese, viewing this aggressive neighbor with justifiable alarm. Thus, China had closed the door to Pan Am as well.

To circumvent the problem, Trippe moved to secure landing rights at the British Crown colony of Hong Kong, just off the Chinese mainland. At the same time Trippe made plans to purchase a part ownership in China's interior airline, the China National Aviation Corporation. Established in 1930 by the Curtiss-Wright Company, CNAC had by 1932 fallen on hard times, and was in danger of losing its important Shanghai-Canton route.

The Chinese government held majority ownership of CNAC. The remaining 45 percent was now owned by North American Aviation. In January of 1933, Trippe sent Harold M. Bixby, a long-time associate and Pan Am vice president, to China to negotiate the purchase of North American's interest and to see what could be done to rebuild the airline into a functioning, profit-making operation. After six months of often difficult negotiating, Bixby was able to secure the minority ownership for Trippe, and Trippe's dream of a California-China route became a reality.

Before regular Clipper service could be established, the China National Aviation Corporation (whose name translated literally as the Middle Kingdom Space Machine Family) had to be rebuilt from the ground up. Trippe and the Chinese government saw to it that new weather and radio stations and new airports were built. CNAC purchased new aircraft and drew up schedules into interior China.

In 1937, Pan Am secured landing rights at Hong Kong. A regular schedule of M-130 flights to Manila was established. Pan Am also employed an S-42 on the Manila-Hong Kong route for several years, while DC-2 and DC-3 aircraft made the flight from Kai-tak Airport at Hong Kong to airports on the Chinese mainland.

Japan invaded China in 1937, quickly making a regular schedule of commercial flights an impossible task. CNAC aircraft came under Japanese fire on more than one occasion, and were even shot down, despite the fact that America had not yet entered the war. Japanese hostilities toward American and other western interests in China continued to increase until the massive attack on Pearl Harbor and other American outposts in the Pacific in December of 1941.

On Dec. 8, the Japanese attacked Hong Kong and within days the British colony capitulated. Although CNAC lost a number of aircraft in the attack, the airline continued to fly into China from Burma and later from India. Throughout the war, CNAC provided a vital link between China and the outside world.

Pan Am's involvement with CNAC ended in 1949 with the establishment of communist rule in China.

The Shanghai terminal of CNAC, 1930s.

PAA

The famous DC-2½ of CNAC. This DC-3 lost a wing to a Japanese air attack in the late 1930s and was forced to land. There were no spare DC-3 wings to fix the plane, only a DC-2 wing stored 800 miles away. William Langhorne Bond, who ran CNAC for Pan Am and the Chinese government ordered the DC-2 wing flown to the downed aircraft and attached in hopes it would get the plane off the ground. It miraculously worked and the DC-3 took off and flew to its destination.   PAA

HUGO LEUTERITZ

As Pan Am pushed routes further and further into previously unflown skies, the airline came to owe an increasing debt to the ingenuity of one man—Hugo Leuteritz. Radio communications were primitive in the early part of the twentieth century. Leuteritz provided Juan Trippe with the innovations in communications that enabled Pan Am to stay at the forefront of commercial aviation development.

Leuteritz had begun tinkering with radios as early as 1910. In 1919, he went to work for a newly formed company, the Radio Corporation of America, where he began to apply radio communications and navigation to the new field of aviation. Ships were using radio. Leuteritz reasoned that airplanes could do the same.

The biggest obstacle to the use of radio communications in the field of aviation was the weight of the necessary equipment. RCA began by designing a transmitter small enough to fit aboard an airplane, yet powerful enough to be of service. The passage of time saw many more advancements in radio science, as often as not stamped with the Leuteritz imprint, as in the pioneering of ground-based direction finders to help guide an airplane on its proper course.

In the late 1920s, Leuteritz left RCA and went to work for Pan Am, where he directed the construction of state-of-the-art direction finders and radio installations across the Pacific, enabling Pan Am's pilots to find their way from one tiny island to another. Pioneering radio facilities throughout the world, Leuteritz served Pan Am as chief of communications until 1946.

CAPTAIN EDWIN C. MUSICK

If there is an unsung hero in the history of aviation, surely it is Pan American's first pilot, Edwin C. Musick. Of many "firsts" credited to him, the one for which he is best known is the airmail flight from San Francisco to Manila on Nov. 22-29, 1935. However, this flight is but one episode from a career of first flights that stretched over a period of more than 20 years.

Born in St. Louis, Missouri, in 1894, Musick learned to fly at a commercial flying school in Los Angeles before America's entry into World War I. In 1917 he joined the Army Air Corps at San Diego as a civilian flight instructor, a position he retained during the war, teaching at airfields near Wichita Falls, Texas, and Miami, Florida. At the end of the war, Musick embarked on his own flying business in Florida, where he became one of the first pilots to accumulate 10,000 hours of flying time.

In October of 1927, Musick joined Juan Trippe's fledgling airline, Pan American Airways, and made the inaugural airmail flight from Key West, Florida, to Havana, Cuba, in a Fokker tri-motor. Musick pioneered new routes to the Caribbean and then on to South America, at times teaming up with Col. Charles A. Lindbergh, then a technical consultant to Pan American.

In 1930 Musick became chief pilot of Pan Am's Caribbean Division, and his real work on over-water flying began. The Caribbean operation, an important service in its own right, also served as a flying laboratory for development of special techniques of over-ocean flying. Here the airline hoped to perfect the concept of a departmentalized flight crew, and to further develop multi-engine aircraft, a meteorological service, communications, flight control and equipment maintenance.

When the Sikorsky S-42 was accepted by Pan American, Trippe assigned Musick to be the pilot for the plane's trial flights. In a series of rigorous tests, Musick set 10 world records for seaplane performance, records previously held by pilots from Europe. At one time, Musick held claim to more officially recognized world records than did any other pilot in the U.S. or abroad.

After exhaustive tests in the Caribbean, the S-42 was flown to California for four survey flights over the trans-Pacific route. Musick piloted the first two survey flights. Shortly thereafter, in 1935-36, he pioneered the Martin 130 airmail and passenger flights from California to Manila.

Again in an S-42, Musick pioneered a new route from San Francisco to Honolulu, Kingman Reef, American Samoa and New Zealand in March of 1937.

The end of this remarkable flying career came tragically on Jan. 11, 1938, when the *Samoan Clipper* NC16734, an S-42B, disappeared on a survey flight from Pago Pago, American Samoa, to Auckland, New Zealand. Apparently the Clipper exploded in mid-air as the crew attempted to dump her fuel for an emergency landing back at Pago Pago. Neither the plane nor the six crewmen were ever found, only some debris, despite an extensive search.

Although his untimely death prevented him from sharing his experience as a pilot and an instructor of pilots during World War II, a Liberty Ship was named in his honor and christened by his widow, Cleo, at the Kaiser Shipyard in Richmond, California. More than anyone's, Edwin C. Musick's name would remain synonymous with the early development of America's largest overseas airline.

Capt. Edwin C. Musick.   PAA

Flying between San Diego and San Francisco on the *China Clipper* in November 1935, William Burke Miller of NBC and Capt. Musick converse with Captains Albert W. Stevens and Orvil A. Anderson in the *Explorer II*. Stevens and Anderson were establishing a world balloon record, ascending nearly fourteen miles into the stratosphere above South Dakota.

PAA

On Nov. 21, 1958, two of the original crew of the early survey flights, Harry C. Canaday (left) and Wilson T. Jarboe, Jr., met with Mrs. Edwin Musick at Clipper Hall in Long Island City, New York. PAA

Musick becomes famous world-wide with his portrait on the cover of the Dec. 2, 1935, issue of *Time* magazine.

PAA

Igor Sikorsky began building multi-engine airplanes before the first World War. In 1931, he completed his first four-engine amphibian, the S-40 *American Clipper*, which would be christened by Mrs. Herbert Hoover. The design of this plane, destined for the growing Pan American Airways System, was much influenced by Sikorsky's technical advisor Charles A. Lindbergh.

A great amount of work, research and experimentation went into the development of the S-40. Theory, design, and stress analysis required the full efforts of the Sikorsky organization for more than two years. From its first flight, the S-40 was a success, capable of carrying forty passengers over a considerable distance. Yet aviation technology was changing rapidly in these years, and on the maiden flight of the S-40, from Miami to the Panama Canal, Sikorsky and Lindbergh were already discussing the design of the next generation of flying boats.

Thus the S-42 was born, the first true Clipper, which would pave the way for trans-Pacific flights later to be dominated by the M-130 and the B-314 flying boats. Although contracts were granted for the S-42 and the M-130 at about the same time, the S-42 (which at the time of its construction would be the largest commercial flying boat in existence), came off the assembly line first. The S-42 was a major improvement over the S-40 series, with a range, fully loaded, of 1,200 miles and a maximum range, carrying an 800-pound payload of 3,000 miles.

Sikorsky constructed his entire plane of duralumin, with the exception of the tail surfaces and the wing aft of the rear spar; these components were fabric covered. Eight elliptical tanks between the spars held a total of 1,240 gallons of fuel. Watertight bulkheads divided the hull into nine compartments: anchor locker, crew quarters, two holds, which could be converted to accommodate passengers, four passenger cabins seating eight, and a rear luggage hold. The crew of five consisted of two pilots, an engineer, a radio operator, and a steward, and the plane could carry up to 32 passengers.

The wing was built in one piece. The center section carried four Pratt and Whitney Hornet R-1690, S3D1-G engines. The propellers were three-bladed, controllable pitch, Hamilton Standards, with all pitch-control mechanisms synchronized from the cockpit.

The pilot's compartment seated the pilot and co-pilot, the radio operator, and the flight mechanic (engineer). Here controls were divided between the pilot's area and that of the mechanic much the same as in today's multi-engine aircraft.

Adjustable passenger seats hung from the bulkheads, eliminating chair legs. Two completely equipped toilets were built into each plane, along with the necessary steward's equipment. And for passengers interested in the view, three circular windows were built into the exterior bulkheads of the passenger compartments.

Every external part of the hull could be reached by a center-ridge walkway that extended from bow to stern. This walkway, along with the wing walkways and the engine platforms, made it possible to conduct almost any inspection or service operation without a need for outside scaffolding.

Upon consideration of the conditions under which the S-42 would operate, Sikorsky designed the plane with a high wing loading, thirty pounds per square inch. The S-42 would primarily be flown at high cruis-

Aviation designer Igor Sikorsky and Capt. Edwin Musick, Pan Am's pioneer pilot.   PAA

Forerunners of the S-42. Top: S-41. Bottom: S-40.

Top: GW   Bottom: PAA

ing speeds over transoceanic routes. Routes of this type would have no intermediate landing possibilities, and in view of the distances and duration of flight, the planes would have to withstand extreme weather conditions. Good airworthiness in stormy weather was essential, and Sikorsky's aerodynamic study showed that the action of a squall or of a vertical air gust became more violent as the wing loading decreased.

The disadvantages of heavy wing loading, namely, difficult takeoff and fast landing, were avoided by the use of a specially designed, high-lift, hydraulic flap. After careful wind-tunnel study of several designs, Sikorsky chose a straight flap that filled up the rear of the wing between the ailerons.

Flight tests confirmed his design theory. The S-42 flew easily and smoothly in the roughest of weather. The relatively small and rigid wing had the added advantage of weathering strong winds and heavy squalls while afloat.

The S-42 paved the way for over-ocean flights that would carry passengers and cargo throughout the world. For Pan Am, Sikorsky's plane would fly all the north and south Pacific survey flights, from 1935-1937, and would later provide shuttle service from Manila to Hong Kong.

An S-42B at the Sikorsky plant.   UT

The Hornet-powered S-42 flying over Bridgeport, Conn. The Sikorsky plant is in the upper right on the waterfront.   UT

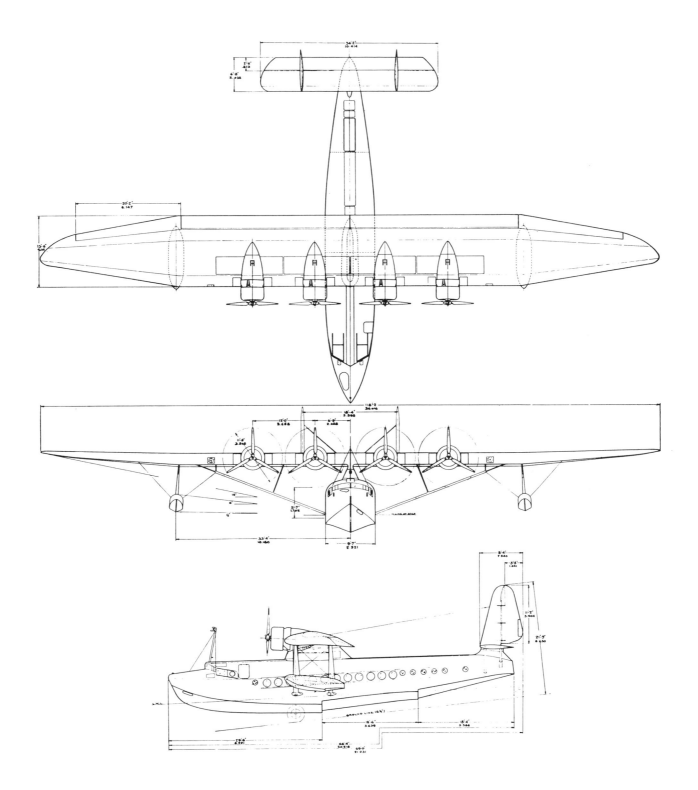

Line drawing of the S-42. Production by the Sikorsky Aircraft Company, Connecticut, began in 1934.

UT

An S-42B in the maintenance hangar at Alameda.   GW

An S-42 ready for service in the Pacific. The wheels could be attached for beaching purposes.   UT

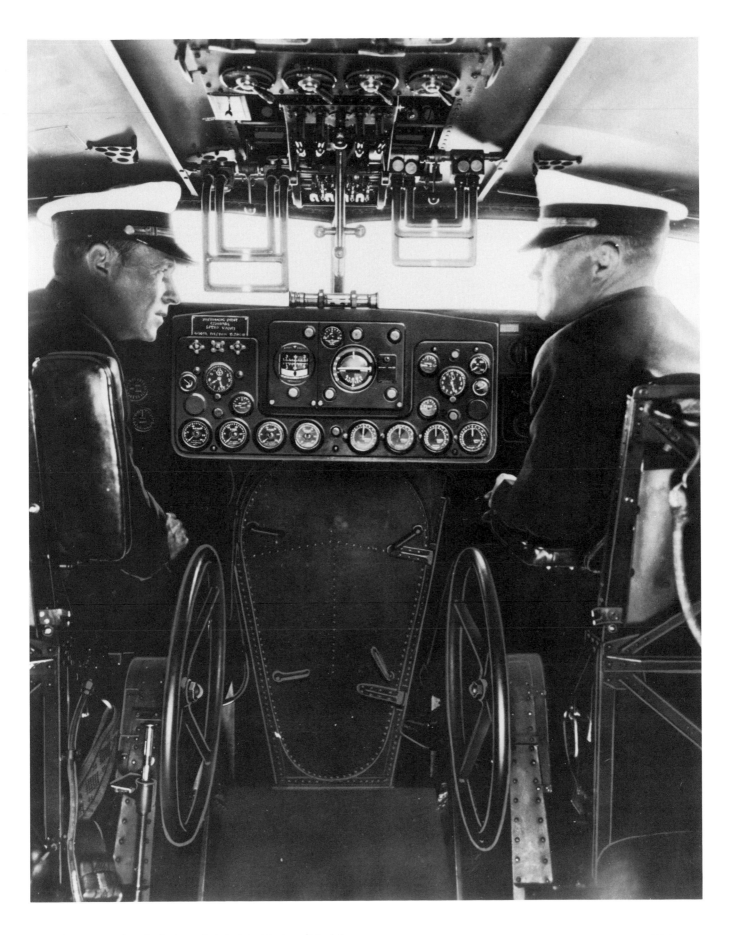

The interior of an S-42. Capt. Edwin Musick sits on the left.   PAA

Casting off from the Alameda
base.   GW

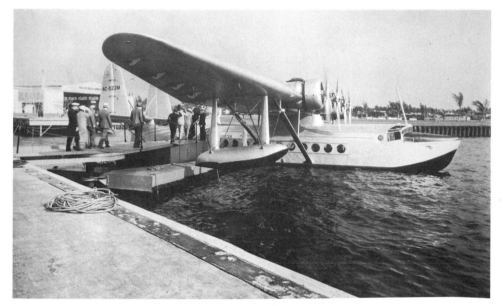

Passengers embark on an
S-42.   PAA

An S-42 flys over the towers
of the Golden Gate Bridge in
San Francisco. The bridge's
cables and deck had yet to be
completed. This was on the
April 1935 survey flight.
                          UT

An S-42 at the Ford Island Naval Air Station, Pearl Harbor, Hawaii. Pan Am used this facility from 1935 to 1940.   NA

Bow view of the *Hong Kong Clipper* at Pearl Harbor, 1937. This S-42B flew the shuttle route between Manila and Hong Kong.
NA

The *China Clipper* over San Francisco.   PAA

CHAPTER FOUR

MARTIN M-130

No sooner had the contract been awarded for the S-42 than Pan Am realized the long, trans-ocean routes—in particular the Pacific route—would require an even larger plane. Six companies expressed an interest in designing and manufacturing a new flying boat. However, only two, the Glenn L. Martin Company of Middle River, Md., and the Sikorsky Company, had the capability to compete for this new Pan Am contract. In spite of Sikorsky's previous success with the S-42, the Martin Company won the day.

The new plane would need a maximum range of more than 2,400 miles (the distance from San Francisco to Hawaii, the longest leg of the trans-Pacific route), and it would have to fly those miles carrying enough passengers, mail and other cargo to make the route financially rewarding. Roughly speaking, the plane would be called upon to carry cargo equal to her own gross weight.

Pan Am provided the Martin Company with the new plane's specifications, and assisted in each step of the plane's design and construction. Chief engineer Lassiter Milbur, assistant chief engineer and test pilot Ken Ebel, and project engineer L.D. McCarthy were given much of the responsibility for the birth of the new flying boat.

The Middle River, Md., plant of the Glenn L. Martin Company, manufacturer of the M-130 flying boat, 1931.

J.M. Murphy, Martin Marietta, Denver, Colo.

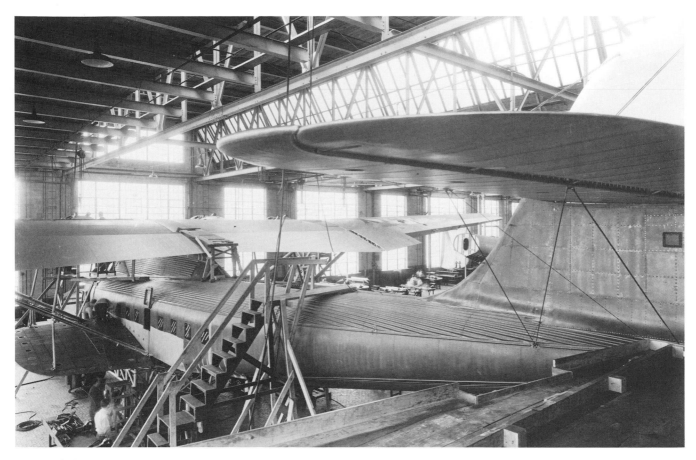

Inside the Martin plant, workers construct the giant M-130. PAA

Looking up from the flight mechanic's conning tower.
PAA

Looking forward from the flight mechanic's seat.   PAA

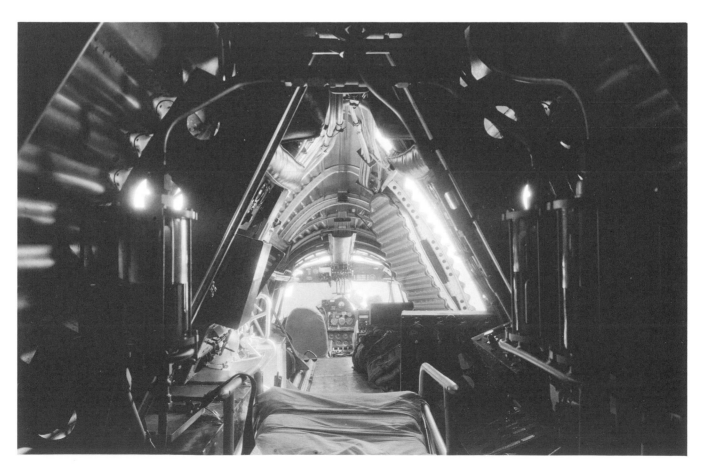

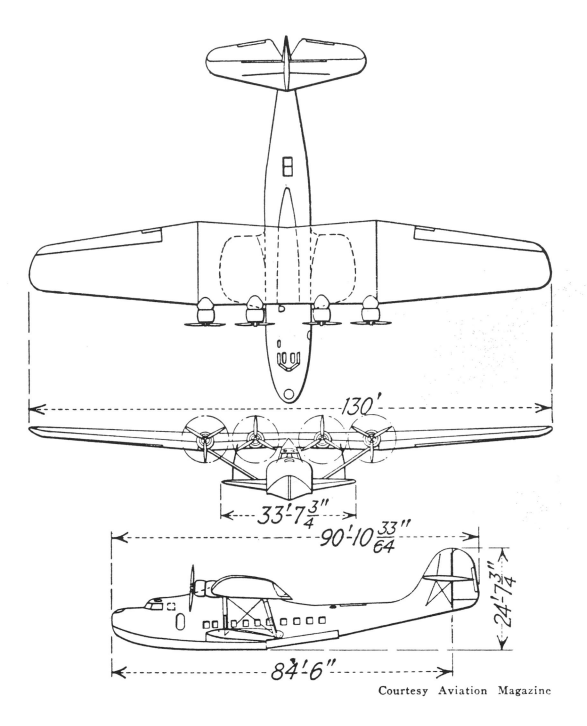

Courtesy Aviation Magazine

THE GLENN L. MARTIN COMPANY
Baltimore, Md.
MARTIN 130 ——— 14-50 PLACE
ENGINES: FOUR PRATT & WHITNEY TWIN WASPS

The famous Pacific Clippers of the Pan American Airways fleet are by far the largest aircraft on the world's airways. Huge twenty-six-ton giants, built by Martin, they were designed to meet every rigid requirement ocean air transport operation might demand. As fleet as the wind, they are as staunch as an ocean liner. The great ninety-foot hull is divided into six water-tight compartments, any two of which are capable of keeping the ship afloat under any conceivable conditions. The spreading one hundred and thirty-foot wing mounts four huge engines of a thousand horsepower each—equivalent to that of an ordinary locomotive. Marvels of mechanical efficiency, nearly half of this four thousand horsepower is constantly in reserve at all cruising speeds. The big three-bladed propellers even shift their pitch automatically to assure utmost efficiency. On the Flight Deck is the bridge, on which two pilot-officers are on duty at all times; the radio officer, who is in constant touch with at least two ground stations, who is in periodic contact with every ship on the sea below, and who exchanges bearings every few minutes between the Clipper and the guarding radio Direction-Finding stations at each base. Further aft, in his cabane near the edge of the huge wing, and in line with the powerful engines, the Engineering Officer controls the mechanical operation of the giant ship and maintains a constant guard over the great power plants, through one hundred and eighty-one instruments, levers and valves.

On the Main Deck forward is the buffet, from which all meals aloft are served. Also, the main cargo holds, and the air-conditioning system. No matter what the outside temperature, or what the height at which you are flying, the Clipper is constantly maintained at a proper, and pleasant temperature. Next is the Navigation Officer's cabin, where are kept the remarkable instruments with which the course of the ship is plotted, a map case, master compass, and chronometer. Here, too, are berths for the flying officers who are "Off Watch," rest chairs, and the Captain's desk. Next are the roomy, soundproofed, thoroughly air-conditioned passenger cabins. First the lounge, where as many as fifteen passengers may be accommodated comfortably. So effectively are the walls soundproofed that a normal conversational tone may be used at all times. Large, spacious, airy cabins are conducive to restfulness and ease of movement. Passengers may—and constantly do—move about the ship at will. The lounge itself is as large as a good-sized living room. Next to the lounge are two standard cabins with berths for twelve sleeping passengers, or lounge chairs for twenty for the shorter daylight flights between the Islands. Aft of these are located the dressing rooms and further aft, additional cargo holds and complete emergency equipment. Aboard these famous flying boats you will find every comfort and convenience you would expect on the finest ocean liners. And a service which no other form of transport can provide.

Inside the Martin plant, workers construct the giant M-130.
                                                    PAA

Installing engines at the Martin plant, 1935.   PAA

The PAA acceptance crew poses with representatives of the Hamilton Prop Co., Pratt and Whitney, and the Martin Co., at the Martin factory on Oct. 7, 1935. The *China Clipper*, NC-14716, first to be delivered, is in the background. Rear, left to right: Max Weber, Ralph Dahlstrom, Sam P. Crago, Capt. Edwin Musick, William Miller, Ralph Beecher, C. Wright. Front, left to right: T. Ray Runnells, Floyd Penning, J.C. McCarty.   PAA

MODEL 130
THE MARTIN OCEAN TRANSPORT

The Martin M-130 was an all-metal, high-wing, flying boat with a 130-foot span, powered by four Pratt & Whitney R-1830-geared, air-cooled radial engines. It had luxurious accommodations for 46 passengers as a day transport, and was convertible into an 18-30 passenger night transport with large, comfortable berths. As a passenger plane, the transport carried a crew of seven. The M-130 was also convertible into a mail plane, upon removal of the passenger equipment, having a range of over 4,000 miles.

The hull was subdivided into the following compartments:

a—A forward anchor compartment.

b—A control room for the pilots, including the radio operator's station, with a mail and cargo compartment beneath the floor on the starboard side.

c—A baggage compartment on the starboard side, with an entrance hatch and a galley on the port side.

d—A forward passenger compartment accommodating 10 passengers.

e—A flight mechanic's station located immediately forward of the leading edge of the wing above the forward passenger compartment.

f—A lounge compartment accommodating 16 passengers.

g—Two rear compartments accommodating 10 passengers each.

h—A toilet located on both sides and a steward's office on the port side.

i—A rear entrance hatch in the deck, leading into a compartment for baggage.

The control bridge was equipped with dual flight controls and instruments, including a Sperry Automatic Pilot. The radio operator's station was immediately behind the pilot on the starboard side, within easy speaking distance of either pilot. A hatch was installed in the deck of the pilothouse for emergency exit and to facilitate directing mooring operations. A compartment for mail and cargo was provided beneath the pilotroom floor.

The M-130, X-14714, first of the clippers, rolls out of the Martin hangar at Middle River on Nov. 30, 1934.   PAA

An entrance hatch equipped with hinged doors was situated on the port side immediately aft of the pilot-house. A completely equipped galley was located adjacent to the entrance hatch on the port side.

The flight mechanic's station was located above the forward passenger compartment, in the cabin, and windows were installed to give clear vision of all engine housings. A complete set of power plant instruments for each of the four engines was installed at this station.

The passenger compartments were furnished with large, comfortable seats, convertible into berths, and equipment such as magazine racks and tables were included in the passenger accommodations. Curtains for the night sleeping arrangement were installed in each compartment.

The lounge was equipped with several individual chairs, in addition to the fixed seats, and was large and roomy. Emergency exits for the passenger compartments were provided by the two rear windows, one on each side, in the lounge compartment.

A noteworthy feature of the plane was the hull and seawing (or sponsons) combination. The seawings were primarily intended to produce lateral stability on the water, which purpose they accomplished better than outboard floats. In addition to their primary function of providing lateral stability, the seawings also carried 950 gallons of fuel each, in tanks built integraly with their structure. The seawings held down the spray and water usually thrown up into the tail surfaces, and derived useful lift from the bow wave. The top surfaces and tips of the seawings were of an airfoil shape, producing an additional aerodynamic lifting area. The hull was of the two-step, deep "V" type, with a pronounced reverse curvature forward of the main step, producing high water reactions at the

beginning of the takeoff run and causing the boat to rise to main step quickly.

The hull was constructed of riveted 24ST aluminum alloy, consisting of transverse bulkheads and frames, supplementary keelson, corrugated bottom skin and deck covering, and smooth side skin. Longitudinal stringers were not employed in the hull construction, the necessary strength being obtained by the deck and bottom corrugations. The hull was provided with four watertight bulkheads. The seawings were of riveted 24ST aluminum alloy construction with longitudinal and transverse framing and corrugated bottom skin and smooth top skin. The fittings attaching the seawings to the hull were machined from solid steel bars.

The wing consisted of a braced center section and two cantilever outer panels of riveted 24ST aluminum alloy construction. The primary structure was of the box girder type, with tension field web beams acting as side members. The bottom covering was smooth stressed skin and the top covering was corrugated sheet, with corrugations parallel to the span, and covered with thin smooth sheet. Stiffeners were added to the beam webs and former ribs supported the corrugations. The nose ribs and metal leading edge covering were attached to the rear beam. The ailerons were balanced and had metal framework and fabric covering. Trailing edge tabs were installed on the ailerons, adjustable from the pilots' cockpit, to overcome any tendency toward wing heaviness. All highly stressed wing fittings were of chrome molybdenum steel.

The tail surfaces were of the monoplane type, with single fin and rudder. The fin was in two sections: a lower metal-covered stub fin built integraly with the hull structure, and an upper fabric-covered detachable section of metal framework. The rudder was provided with a trailing edge tab adjustable from the pilots' cockpit, to counteract the unbalanced thrust when flying with any one engine dead. The stabilizer

Formal presentation of the *China Clipper* at the Martin plant, Oct. 9, 1935. A Department of Commerce license was presented to Capt. Musick by Juan Trippe.

Alan Wright

was of riveted 24ST aluminum alloy framework, fabric covered, and was rigidly attached to the stub fin by steel fittings. Fore and aft trim was accomplished by means of trailing edge tabs on the elevator, adjustable from the pilots' cockpit. The elevators were of riveted 24ST aluminum alloy framework and were fabric covered, as was the rudder. All control wires, horns, etc., were of the internal type. The leading edges of all tail surfaces were metal covered. The tail surfaces were braced to the hull by streamline stainless steel wires.

The M-130 was powered with four Pratt & Whitney R-1830-geared, air-cooled radial engines equipped with Hamilton-Standard constant speed controllable propellers. The engine housings, or nacelles, were fully cowled and interchangeable. Immediately aft of the engine accessories, a firewall of aluminum alloy and stainless steel construction was installed. The oil was carried in four tanks, one in each nacelle behind the firewall, accommodating 57 gallons each. The fuel was carried in two auxiliary tanks installed in the wing center section, and in tanks built integral with the hull and seawing structure. The two wing tanks held 100 gallons each, and seawings 950 gallons each, and the two hull tanks 750 gallons and 1,230 gallons respectively, making a total fuel capacity of 4,080 gallons. Oil turbine driven pumps were employed to transfer the fuel from the hull and seawing tanks to the wing tanks. A water separator was installed in the fuel system to eliminate the possibility of water getting into the carburetors through the fuel system.

Particular attention was paid to the incorporation of superior maintenance features throughout the plane.

Due to the riveted type of construction used throughout the airplane, a minimum of maintenance was required. Doors were provided in the hull floor and in the wing panels and tail surfaces to facilitate inspection and maintenance of the control, electrical and fuel systems. Manholes were incorporated in the seawings to provide easy access to all parts of their interior structure. Lubrication fittings were installed on all moving parts of the power plant and control surface systems and wherever possible self-lubricating ball bearings were incorporated. To facilitate maintenance of the engines and power plant accessories, two working platforms were provided for each nacelle, one on each side. These platforms folded into the leading edge of the wing, and when unfolded, provided a strong and convenient means for engine and accessory maintenance and repair.

The structure was carefully finished with protective coatings against corrosion. All aluminum alloy parts were anodized and painted prior to final assembly, and steel parts were cadmium plated. Particular care was taken regarding the assembly of dissimilar metals by incorporating impregnated fabric between these parts.

As these were strictly on-the-water planes, a movable carriage was designed to haul them out of the water and up to a hangar area.

Construction began in November of 1932 at the Middle River, Md., plant and the first keel, which would belong to the *Hawaii Clipper*, was set in 1933. Pan Am authorized three planes in 1934 at an approximate cost of $430,000 apiece.

The only visit by a Clipper to Avalon Harbor, Catalina Island, off the California coast was in 1937.   PAA

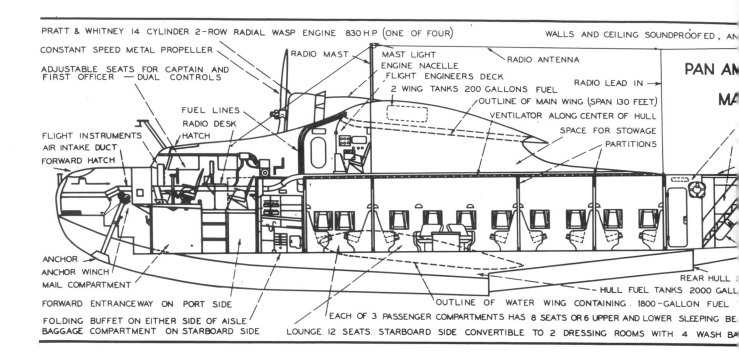

PRATT & WHITNEY 14 CYLINDER 2-ROW RADIAL WASP ENGINE 830 H.P. (ONE OF FOUR)
CONSTANT SPEED METAL PROPELLER
ADJUSTABLE SEATS FOR CAPTAIN AND FIRST OFFICER — DUAL CONTROLS
FUEL LINES
RADIO DESK
HATCH
FLIGHT INSTRUMENTS
AIR INTAKE DUCT
FORWARD HATCH
ANCHOR
ANCHOR WINCH
MAIL COMPARTMENT
FORWARD ENTRANCEWAY ON PORT SIDE
FOLDING BUFFET ON EITHER SIDE OF AISLE
BAGGAGE COMPARTMENT ON STARBOARD SIDE

RADIO MAST
MAST LIGHT
ENGINE NACELLE
FLIGHT ENGINEERS DECK
2 WING TANKS 200 GALLONS FUEL
RADIO ANTENNA
RADIO LEAD IN
OUTLINE OF MAIN WING (SPAN 130 FEET)
VENTILATOR ALONG CENTER OF HULL
SPACE FOR STOWAGE
PARTITIONS

WALLS AND CEILING SOUNDPROOFED, AN
PAN AM
MA

REAR HULL
HULL FUEL TANKS 2000 GALL
OUTLINE OF WATER WING CONTAINING 1800-GALLON FUEL
EACH OF 3 PASSENGER COMPARTMENTS HAS 8 SEATS OR 6 UPPER AND LOWER SLEEPING BE
LOUNGE 12 SEATS. STARBOARD SIDE CONVERTIBLE TO 2 DRESSING ROOMS WITH 4 WASH BA

The Martin Motor Stand provided easy access to the four engines of the *Philippine Clipper*. This photo was probably taken at the Alameda base.

PAA

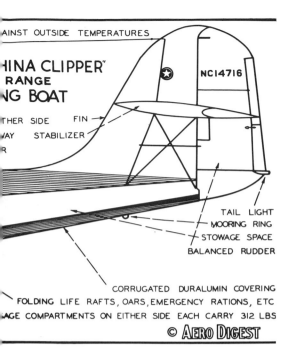

AINST OUTSIDE TEMPERATURES

"HINA CLIPPER"
RANGE
NG BOAT

THER SIDE — FIN →
WAY — STABILIZER
R

NC14716

TAIL LIGHT
MOORING RING
STOWAGE SPACE
BALANCED RUDDER

CORRUGATED DURALUMIN COVERING
FOLDING LIFE RAFTS, OARS, EMERGENCY RATIONS, ETC
AGE COMPARTMENTS ON EITHER SIDE EACH CARRY 312 LBS

© AERO DIGEST

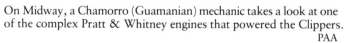

On Midway, a Chamorro (Guamanian) mechanic takes a look at one of the complex Pratt & Whitney engines that powered the Clippers.

PAA

With a clipper on the water, mechanics required special arrangements to gain access to her engines.   PAA

The M-130 cockpit.   PAA

A local Baltimore newspaper gave a glowing description of the new Martin flying boat.

BOAT BROUGHT OUT OF PLANT

Largest Craft of Kind Ever Built In U.S. Leaves Assembly Room

VISITORS SEE SHIP AT MIDDLE RIVER

Designed To Carry Forty-Six Passengers And Freight

A streamlined mass of shining silver and black, the largest flying boat ever built on the American continent, was brought out into the open, all slicked up, and had her motors turned over for the first time this afternoon at the plant of the Glenn L. Martin Company, where she grew from a mass of blue prints.

The ship will not be put into the water today. Officials of the Pan-American Airways, for whom she was built, were present at the Martin plant as the huge vessel emerged from the enormous assembly room into the open.

Facilities for 46 Passengers

Incorporated in the craft are the latest designs, the result of many months' study by aeronautic engineers before a single splinter was fashioned for her building. She is the first of three now under construction at the plant for transatlantic passenger, mail and freight service and is designed to carry forty-six passengers, a crew of four or five, mail and freight. Her useful load is 28,000 pounds, her weight fully loaded is 51,000. As she now stands she is ready for the rigid testing required before she can be turned over to her owners.

During the next week or ten days every section of the ship having to do with motor operation will be tried out in every conceivable way. This, according to officials of the plant, constitutes the "ground test." She will then be put into the water and her flying tests will begin.

Tests Scheduled

The first two or three days of flights will be devoted to giving the test pilot—Kenneth Ebel, assistant chief engineer and chief test pilot at the plant—an opportunity to feel out the ship in the air, at taking off and landing, sharp turns, taxiing, etc. Then the tests required under the contract of building will begin.

These include a speed run and a range run, a test for the time of taking off, a test for the ship's operating power with various motors shut off, her maximum height and other points. The speed run will be over Chesapeake Bay waters, as will other of the tests with the exception of the range run, which will be from Baltimore to Miami, Fla., and return.

The test for speed requires a run of not less than two miles nor more than ten, and the United States Coast and Geodetic Survey has been asked to lay out a course between two navigation points in the bay. These will probably be in the vicinity of Poole's Island and the Craighill channel range lights, it was said, and will give a course of about four miles.

Carries 4,000 Gallons

In the range test the ship, with her gasoline tanks loaded to the maximum capacity of 4,000 gallons of gasoline and sealed, will take off and fly to the Florida city during daylight hours. Remaining there overnight, she will return the next day, making a leisurely trip up the coast. Under the contract she must have a cruising range of slightly over twenty hours, and it is estimated that the two flights will take up between eighteen and nineteen hours, the ship remaining in the air around the bay for the balance of the time.

Sixty seconds has been allowed for the takeoff time of the boat in the contract, but it is believed that she will be able to get away from the water in forty seconds.

The vessel has a wingspread of 130 feet from tip to tip and an overall length of ninety feet. Her four motors, streamlined, are built into the center wing section and, it is said, two of them can keep her in the air. Three can do it easily.

Flying under full load, it is estimated that the four will use 200 gallons of fuel in an hour, with the consumption tapering off as the voyage continues and the load lightens as the fuel is used up. She is designed for a top speed of 180 miles an hour, a cruising speed of 145 miles an hour, at which speed, she will have a range of approximately 3,000 miles. Flying at top speed she will have a range of 2,000 miles and at lower than cruising speed her range can be extended to 4,000 miles.

Other Features Listed

At present she is a shell, with no other accommodations than the two cushioned seats for her pilot and co-pilot away up in the nose. After the tests are completed the work of installing passenger and crew accommodations, soundproofing and other details will be carried out.

Soundproofing engineers have estimated that, when completed, the cabins of the ship will be quieter than a Pullman car. She is built in sections, with water-tight bulkheads and doors capable of shutting off one compartment from another installed. The upper part of her body and her wings have been painted silver, the lower part—that which will come in contact with the water—black. The ship has stubby lower wings which are used as gasoline tanks.

INTERIOR VIEWS

Inside the M-130, passengers were provided comfortable seats, plenty of leg room and ample walking areas. Meals were served on linen-covered tables, and card and board games were available for the asking. On the overnight flight from California to Hawaii, the compartments were converted to provide sleeping quarters for as many as 24 passengers. The flying boats were the ultimate in luxury, the like of which would never be seen again in the air.   PAA

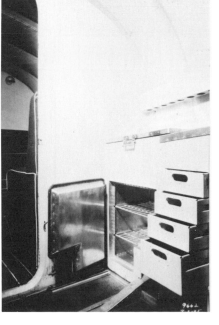

Loading hatch.   PAA   The steward's pantry.   PAA

Time to turn in. Passenger compartments doubled as sleeping quarters. PAA

The tables in the lounge area provided a place to play cards, write letters, and dine.   PAA

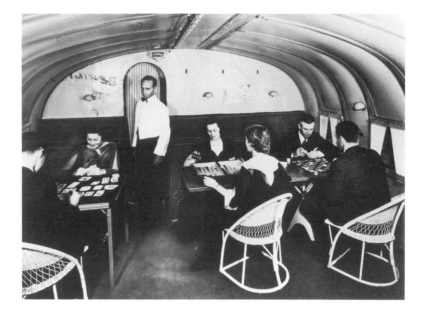

Note: After the M-130s began flying a lot of the fancy wicker chairs, wash-basins, etc., were removed.

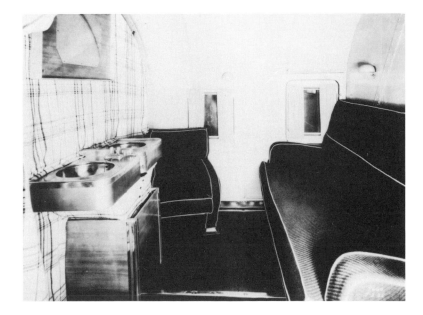

Passenger quarters with dual wash-basins.   PAA

Ken Ebel piloted the NC14716 from the Maryland factory on Dec. 30, 1934. The first clipper, which would be named the *China Clipper,* was delivered to the airline on Oct. 9, 1935. The plane took her name from the country that Juan Trippe hoped his Clippers would open up to world travel, and was nicknamed "Sweet 16" because of the last two digits of her designated number. Two giants of aviation history, Juan Trippe and Charles Lindbergh, took the clipper up for her first flight after acceptance.

The *Philippine Clipper* was delivered on Nov. 14, 1935, and the *Hawaii Clipper* was delivered to Pan Am in March 1936. All three planes were then flown from Baltimore to Pan Am's base at Alameda, Calif., via Miami, Fla., Acapulco, Mexico and San Diego, Calif.

The *China Clipper* became the first M-130 to fly the entire Pacific route to Manila, beginning her journey on Nov. 22, 1935. But in an ironic twist of names of these two planes, the *Philippine Clipper* would be the first flight to Hong Kong, on Oct. 23, 1936.

All three of the M-130 flying boats eventually met tragic ends. The *Hawaii Clipper* was lost in July of 1938 on a routine flight between Guam and Manila. The details of her loss remain a mystery to this day.

There is some evidence that the plane may have been hijacked by the Japanese. (See Ronald W. Jackson's book, *China Clipper*.) Japanese agents would have had at least two good reasons to hijack the *Hawaii Clipper*. The Japanese aviation industry was interested in incorporating some of the features of Pan Am's Clippers into designs of their own flying boats. As added incentive, a shipment of several million dollars destined for the Chinese Nationalists made up part of the *Hawaii Clipper's* cargo on her last flight.

Suspicion might never have been focused on the Japanese had it not been for an earlier incident. Just prior to the maiden flight of the *China Clipper*, in November of 1935, two Japanese nationals were apprehended aboard the plane at Alameda, as they were attempting to sabotage the radio direction finder. Caught before they could do any damage, the two were quietly hustled away to avoid any embarrassing publicity.

In a less mysterious but no less tragic fashion, the *China Clipper* and the *Philippine Clipper* were both lost to accidents during wartime service.

A portable undercarriage was designed to haul the Clippers onto dry land.

PAA

-42-

-43-

PAA

The 1930s were years of great innovation in aircraft design. No sooner did the M-130 come off the production line than Pan Am felt the need for an even larger flying boat, turning again to Sikorsky and Martin and to another major American designer, the Boeing Company.

Founded in 1916 by William E. Boeing as Pacific Aero Products, this company had concentrated on the production of aircraft for military use in the 1930s. The company had not worked on a civilian flying boat since 1929, when it had made final deliveries of its Model 204, a single-engine plane. The Clipper project would not only mark Boeing's re-entrance into the field of civilian flying boats; it would also comprise the largest engineering project yet to be undertaken by the airline.

Discussion of a replacement for the M-130 took place between Boeing's Chief Engineer R.J. Minshull and Pan Am's Vice President Franklin Gledhill in 1935. On February 28, 1936, Pan Am addressed a formal request to Boeing and the Martin Company to submit preliminary studies and proposals for a long-range, four-engine marine aircraft, with engines of from 1,000 to 1,250 horsepower each. During the spring and early summer of that year, Boeing submitted its studies and proposal, and on July 21, 1936, a contract was signed for the construction of six flying boats.

Boeing had been encouraged to bid on the new plane partly because of work recently completed on another giant airplane, the B-15 bomber, also known as the XBLR-1 (Experimental Bomber, Long Range, design 1). For the B-15, Boeing engineers had developed a huge wing span of 149 feet, which they now hoped to adapt to a hull of Pan Am's specifications in order to produce the Model 314.

Towing-basin and wind-tunnel models were prepared and tested during July and August of 1936, and a mockup was completed in September. In February of 1938, the first hull was removed from the jig and weighed, followed by its launching on May 31, 1938. The following week, the plane made her initial runs on Puget Sound, taking to the air for the first time on June 7, 1938. Boeing delivered the first B-314 to Pan Am on January 27, 1939, and on March 26, 1939, the *Yankee Clipper* began a 16,000-mile inspection flight to Europe, prior to scheduled trans-Atlantic service. Serial numbers ran from NC-18601 to NC-18606.

During the summer and fall of 1939, the *Yankee Clipper* underwent extensive testing. Flight tests were conducted carrying gross weights from 55,000 to 82,500 pounds, the greatest weight carried aloft to date by heavier-than-air craft, with the exception of the loads carried by the extinct German *Dornier* DO-X and the Russian *Maxim Gorky.*

Boeing's ocean airliner was a four-engine, high-wing monoplane, with a two-deck hull of semi-monocoque construction and full cantilever wings, tail surfaces and hydrostabilizers. She was the largest passenger-carrying airplane in service anywhere in the world, and the first flying boat to have two flight decks.

Among the features of the Model B-314 were passageways through the wings to each of the four-engine nacelles, affording access to the power plants during flight. On the upper deck the main cargo, mail and baggage holds were positioned aft of the control cabin in the center of the wing stub, below a combination cargo hatch and navigator's observatory. The bow of the hull provided additional cargo space. Mail and cargo holds had a total capacity of five tons.

The passenger deck, designed to simulate the comfort of a modern home, was divided into nine sections with deeply upholstered seats for up to 74 passengers. Berths were available for 36 passengers, 38 if the central lounge was equipped with convertible seats instead of dining tables and chairs. The lounge was the social center of the passenger deck, with tables and chairs for twelve. In addition there were six separate passenger compartments, a specially furnished deluxe compartment, and men's and women's dressing rooms. The two

The *California Clipper* at San Francisco, possibly awaiting her 1939 christening.   GW

Plant No. 1 of the Boeing Company. This plant, where all the 314s were built, was situated south of downtown Seattle, Washington. Here, the portion of the hull between the wing spans, the center section of the wing, and the inboard nacelles, were built as a single unit, providing great strength.   B

WELLWOOD E. BEALL

The father of the world's most elegant flying boat—the Boeing Model 314—Wellwood E. Beall grew up in Colorado in the 1920s, a decade of great advances in aviation technology. In 1930, after earning a bachelor's degree in mechanical engineering and a master's in aeronautical engineering from New York's Guggenheim School of Aeronautics, Beall joined the staff at Boeing's School of Aeronautics in Oakland, California. Two years later he was transferred to Boeing's headquarters in Seattle as a sales engineer.

Soon named Boeing's Far Eastern Sales Manager, Beall went to the Orient, selling airplanes to the Chinese and Philippine governments. Upon his return to the United States in 1936, he learned of Pan Am's request for a new flying boat capable of flying longer distances with a greater payload than the S-42 or the M-130. He was disappointed when Boeing allowed the deadline for bids to pass without submitting one. At the time Boeing was heavily committed to the construction of military aircraft.

Beall's time in the Far East and his appreciation of the great distances to be covered in trans-Pacific air travel convinced him that he and Boeing were uniquely suited to design and build Pan Am's new flying boat. On his own initiative, Beall began preliminary work on the design for such a plane, incorporating the wing of the B-15 bomber recently conceived by Boeing engineers.

With design and data in hand, Beall convinced his superiors at Boeing to ask Pan Am for an extension on the bid deadline. Pan Am agreed, and eventually granted Boeing the contract to build this new generation of flying boats, the B-314.

In the summer of 1936, Beall was named chief engineer on the B-314 project. Directing a team of eleven other engineers, he brought the plane to completion in 1939, after a number of delays due to the complexity and the size of the project. Completion of the B-314 would be just one of many achievements for Beall at Boeing. During his 34-year career with the Boeing Company, Beall was named Chief Engineer (1939), Vice President for Engineering (1943), Vice President for Engineering and Sales (1946), and Senior Vice President (1952), before resigning in 1964. Later, he served the Douglas Aircraft Company as Executive Vice President for Operations. Beall died in 1978.

The official CAA test crew just before going up on one of a series of test flights required for licensing of the plane for Pan Am.   GW

The B-314 test crew in the control bridge, 1939: test pilot Eddie Allen (left) and Joe Boudwin of the CAA.   GW

decks of the airplane were connected by a staircase, and interphone and signal light systems were installed to aid in the crew's efficiency.

Pan Am's requirements called for the new plane to transport a 10,000-pound load 2,400 miles at an altitude of 10,000 feet in the face of a thirty-mile-an-hour headwind while cruising at a speed of 150 miles per hour. The airline also specified that the new Clipper be capable of efficient operation with a minimum of fatigue to the crew, and minimum maintenance. Above all, Pan Am wanted never-before-seen comfort, spaciousness, in fact luxury for its passengers, and Pan Am wanted it packaged in a flying boat that would be as safe as could possibly be made with the existing knowledge of materials and equipment.

In its design criteria, Pan Am stipulated the use of Wright GR-2600-A2 fourteen-cylinder, radial engines and Hamilton-Standard propellers which would be fully feathered—with propeller blades placed edgewise into the slipstream in the event of a shutdown—producing a minimum of drag and preventing engine damage. The Wright Double Cyclone engines undergoing military tests at the time were not a proven power plant when they were selected by Pan Am. However, they ultimately proved to be reliable and powerful engines, producing a burst of 1,500 horsepower each for takeoff. In contrast, the XB-15 bomber, whose wing design had been borrowed for use on the Clipper, was powered by Pratt & Whitney engines which could only generate 1,000 horsepower apiece, a weakness that plagued the

XB-15 throughout its career.

The new Boeing Clipper would be the largest of Pan Am's flying boats, able to carry 4,246 gallons of gasoline and 300 gallons of oil. (Radial aircraft engines were notorious for using great quantities of lubricant.) Every drag-producing protuberance that could rob the plane of speed, range or load capacity had been eliminated. Some flying boats of this era used struts to help brace their large wings. The internal structure gave the XB-15's cantilever wing sufficient strength to support its load without external braces or struts.

The hull of the B-314 was designed to keep the bow wave as clean and low as possible in order to keep the hull dry. Notched steps in the hull bottom, designed to help the clipper break from the surface of the water, were a compromise between ideal water-handling characteristics and aerodynamic streamlining.

Boeing's team of engineers perfected hydrostabilizers —sponsons— in order to keep the clipper balanced on the water. The hydrostabilizers were stub wings mounted on the hull at the waterline, which allowed better high-speed taxiing control than did wing-mounted floats, and were also better suited to rough water. The advantages of sponsons were balanced by their disadvantages of greater weight, higher drag, and their ability to let the flying boats keel over and drag a wingtip on the water's surface in a strong crosswind.

Pan Am contracted for six new flying boats in October of 1939, similar to the original six B-314s placed in service earlier that year. Boeing had improved the plane's fuel efficiency, and the blade design of her large propellers. Takeoff horsepower was increased from

1,500 horsepower to 1,600. The built-in fuel tanks in the hydrostabilizers held an additional 1,200 gallons of gasoline. These changes would allow the Clipper a quicker takeoff and a greater carrying capacity, and would increase the maximum cruising range.

Boeing delivered the first of the new 314s (designated 314-A) on April 20, 1941, and the last on Jan. 20, 1942, just after the United States had entered the second World War. The serial numbers ran from NC-18607 to NC-18612. Boeing then improved the range and performance of the original six, by making changes to their fuel tanks and power plants, changes similar to the innovations designed into the second generation of 314s.

During the war, nine 314s served the United States in both the Atlantic and the Pacific theaters. The other three were sold to the British government. B-314s transported military cargo and troops throughout the world, counting among their passengers the President of the United States and Winston Churchill. Although flown for part of their war service by Pan Am crews, the Clippers had been purchased by the Navy after Pearl Harbor. At war's end, they were offered to Pan Am once again. However, by this time land-based planes had rendered the Clippers obsolete. Mishaps and forced landings at sea would take their toll, and by the early 1950s all twelve of the 314s had sunk or been scrapped.

With their passing, so, too, passed an era of elegance that may never be seen again. All that remains of these flying boats today are a few fragments on display at the Pacific Museum of Flight in Seattle, fittingly, just a short distance from the site of the B-314s' construction.

Construction of the giant B-314 planes at the Boeing plant in 1938. The manufacture of planes this size had never been attempted before.
B and GW

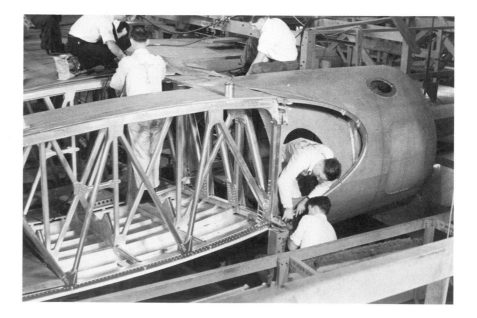

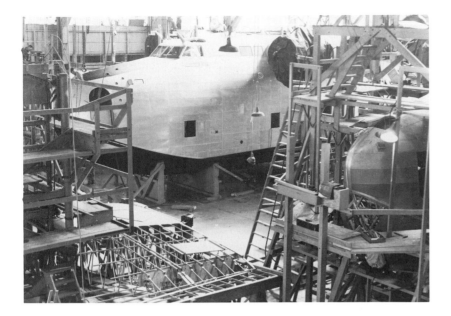

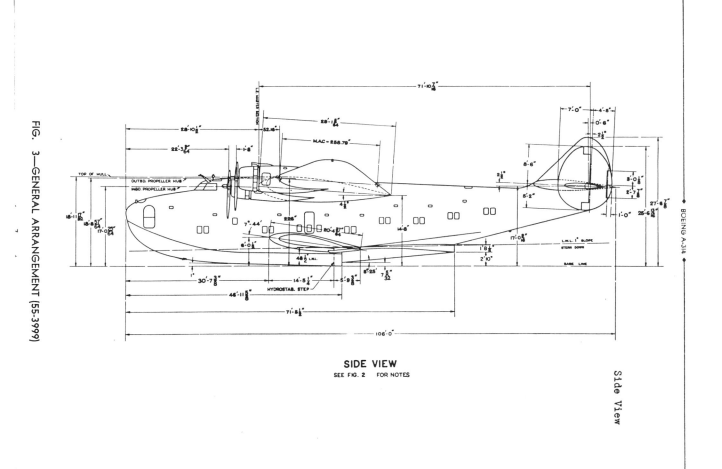

SIDE VIEW

SEE FIG. 2 FOR NOTES

Side View

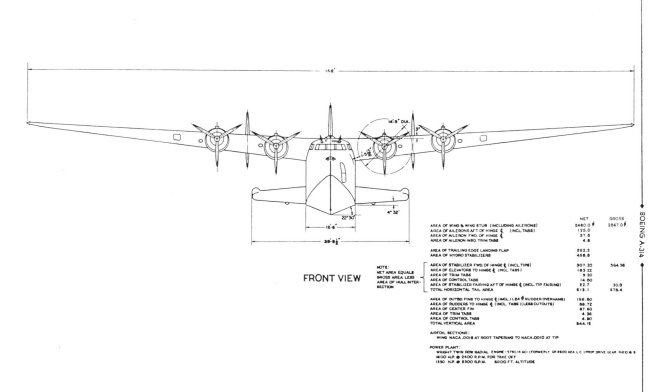

FRONT VIEW

NOTE:
NET AREA EQUALS
GROSS AREA LESS
AREA OF HULL INTER-
SECTION

	NET	GROSS
AREA OF WING & WING STUB (INCLUDING AILERONS)	2480.0 ∮	2867.0 ∮
AREA OF AILERONS AFT OF HINGE ₵ (INCL. TABS)	125.0	
AREA OF AILERON FWD. OF HINGE ₵	37.8	
AREA OF AILERON INBD. TRIM TABS	4.8	
AREA OF TRAILING EDGE LANDING FLAP	252.2	
AREA OF HYDRO STABILIZERS	458.8	
AREA OF STABILIZER FWD. OF HINGE ₵ (INCL. TIPS)	307.20	364.36
AREA OF ELEVATORS TO HINGE ₵ (INCL. TABS)	183.22	
AREA OF TRIM TABS	5.20	
AREA OF CONTROL TABS	14.80	
AREA OF STABILIZER FAIRING AFT OF HINGE ₵ (INCL. TIP FAIRING)	22.7	30.9
TOTAL HORIZONTAL TAIL AREA	513.1	578.4
AREA OF OUTBD. FINS TO HINGE ₵ (INCL. 11.24 ∮ RUDDER OVERHANG)	156.80	
AREA OF RUDDERS TO HINGE ₵ (INCL. TABS)(LESS CUTOUTS)	88.72	
AREA OF CENTER FIN	97.60	
AREA OF TRIM TABS	4.36	
AREA OF CONTROL TABS	4.90	
TOTAL VERTICAL AREA	344.12	

AIRFOIL SECTIONS:
WING NACA .0018 AT ROOT TAPERING TO NACA .0010 AT TIP

POWER PLANT:
WRIGHT TWIN ROW RADIAL ENGINE -579C14 ACI (FORMERLY GR 2600 AEA LC) PROP DRIVE GEAR RATIO 16:9
1600 H.P. @ 2400 R.P.M. FOR TAKE OFF
1350 H.P. @ 2300 R.P.M.   5000 FT. ALTITUDE

-53-

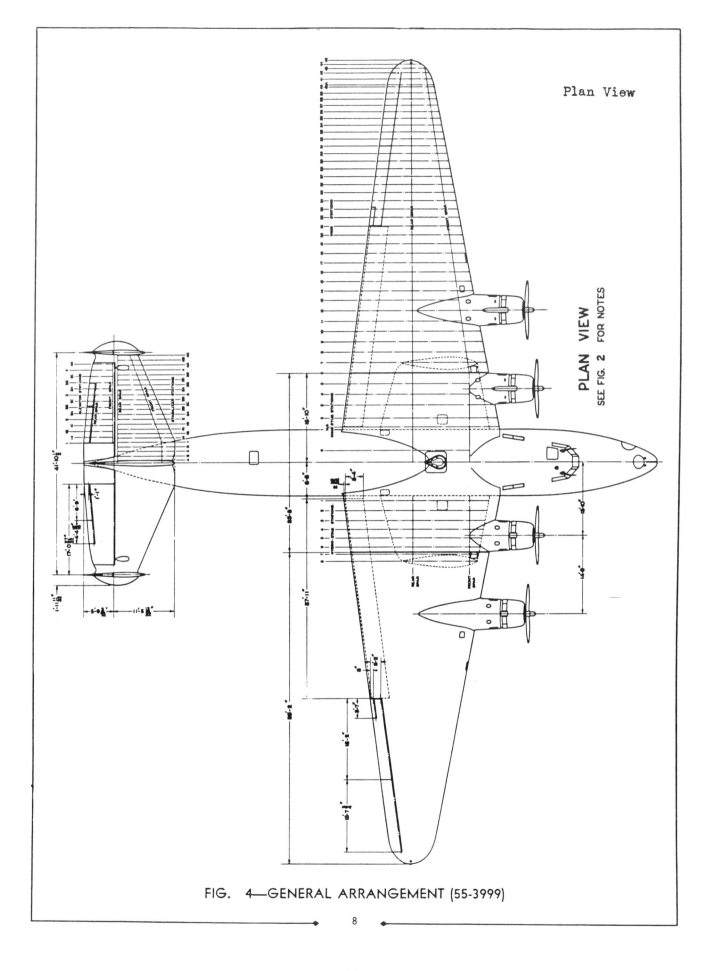

PLAN VIEW
SEE FIG. 2 FOR NOTES

FIG. 4—GENERAL ARRANGEMENT (55-3999)

8

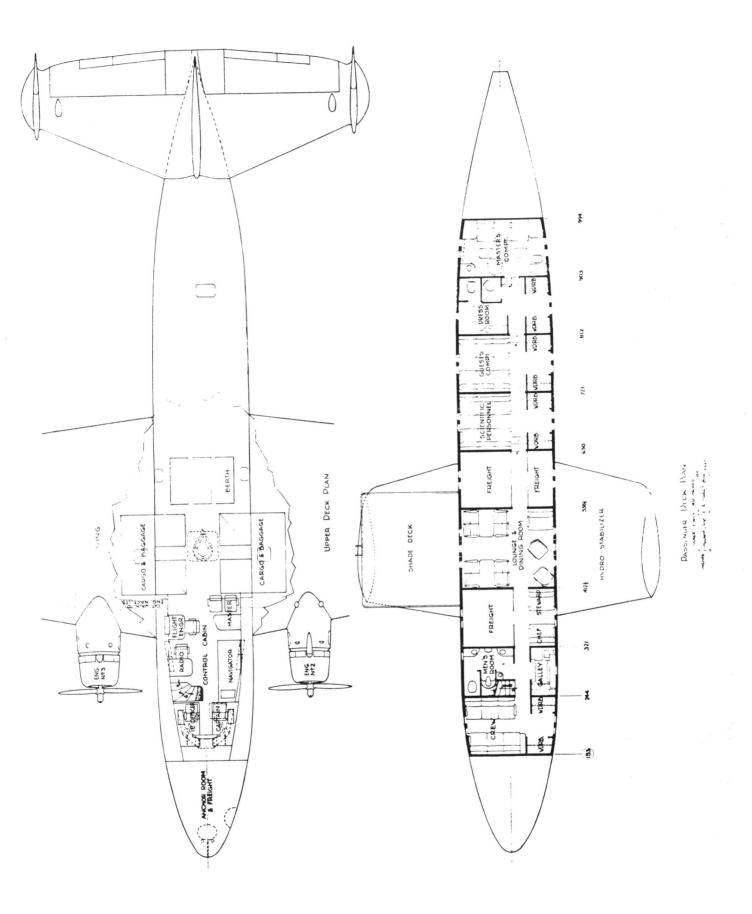

UPPER DECK PLAN

WING

CARGO & BAGGAGE

BERTH

CARGO & BAGGAGE

ENG. NACELLE

ENG. NACELLE

FLIGHT ENGR

RADIO

CONTROL CABIN

MASTER

NAVIGATOR

1ST OFFICER

CAPTAIN

ENG N°3

ENG N°2

ANCHOR ROOM & FREIGHT

PASSENGER DECK PLAN

MASTER'S COMPT

DRESS ROOM

WDRB

WDRB

GUEST'S COMPT

WDRB WDRB

WDRB WDRB

SCIENTIFIC PERSONNEL

WDRB

FREIGHT

FREIGHT

SHADE DECK

LOUNGE & DINING ROOM

HYDRO-STABILIZER

FREIGHT

STEWARD

CHEF

GALLEY

MEN'S ROOM

WDRB

CREW

WDRB

-55-

This center-section slice of the plane is shown being turned over in the process of moving it into the main hull jig. It was built separately and upside down. The structure weighed two tons and there wasn't much clearance for the heel (lower right) or the wing stubs and the inboard engine nacelles (at top). B

NC18601 as she came out of Plant #1. Notice that the prototype only had one tail at this time. One tail proved inadequate, so two tails were tried. Ultimately three tails were installed, the outside ones with movable rudders. In this photo engines are not yet in place. B

Removing the prototype tail on NC18601 in June 1938.
GW

NC18607 and NC18608 coming off the assembly line in early 1941.

GW

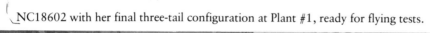

NC18602 with her final three-tail configuration at Plant #1, ready for flying tests.

CONTROL CABIN
BOEING MODEL 314 CLIPPER

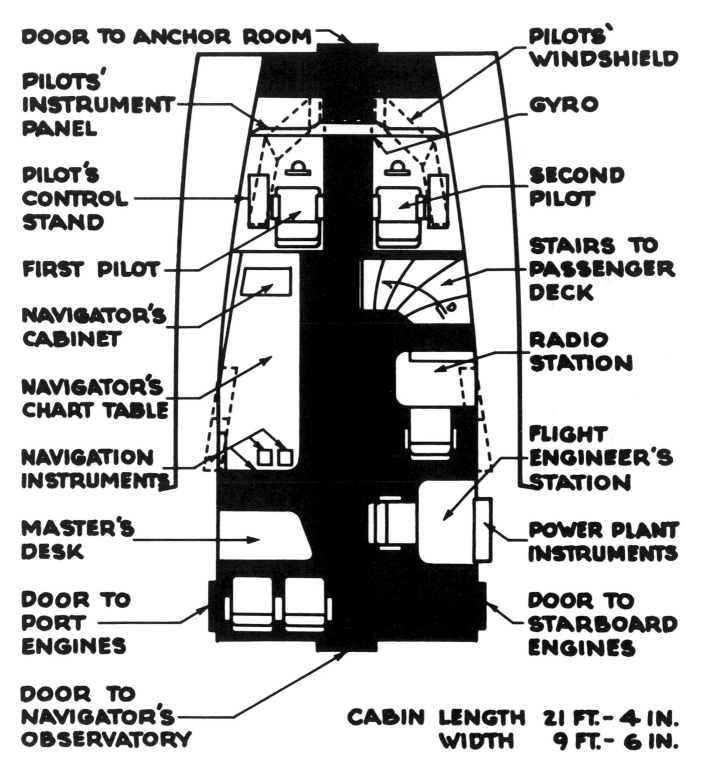

DOOR TO ANCHOR ROOM

PILOTS' WINDSHIELD

PILOTS' INSTRUMENT PANEL

GYRO

PILOT'S CONTROL STAND

SECOND PILOT

FIRST PILOT

STAIRS TO PASSENGER DECK

NAVIGATOR'S CABINET

RADIO STATION

NAVIGATOR'S CHART TABLE

NAVIGATION INSTRUMENTS

FLIGHT ENGINEER'S STATION

MASTER'S DESK

POWER PLANT INSTRUMENTS

DOOR TO PORT ENGINES

DOOR TO STARBOARD ENGINES

DOOR TO NAVIGATOR'S OBSERVATORY

CABIN LENGTH 21 FT. - 4 IN.
WIDTH 9 FT. - 6 IN.

A navigator fixing the position of the plane by "shooting the stars." The navigator's observatory was located just behind the doors to the engines.   B

Catwalk to the engine nacelles.   B

THE CONTROL CABIN

Interior view of the control cabin. The pilots are in the background, the navigator is working at his chart table, the radio operator is directly opposite him and the flight engineer's station is in the foreground.   B

Pilot's instrument panel.　　B

Flight engineer and radio operator's station. The flight engineer took over much of the pilot's power-plant responsibilities.　　B

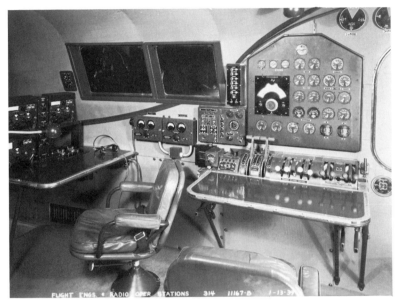

The control cabin.　　B

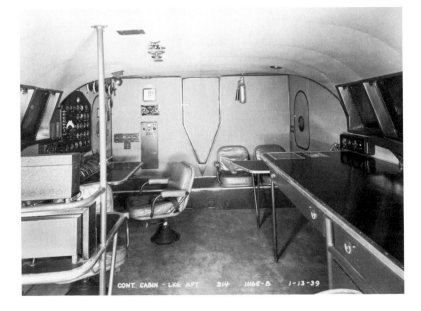

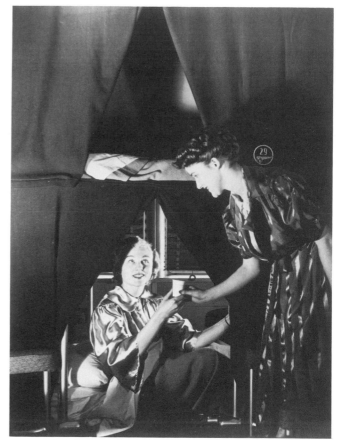

Sleeping berths.   B

INTERIOR OF THE B-314

The B-314 was the ultimate in luxury aircraft, continuing the tradition started by the M-130. Passengers could book a berth for the overnight flight to Honolulu and arrive refreshed the next day. Meals were served on linen-covered tables, and comfortable chairs were provided for all—first class treatment all the way.

B

Dining Salon.   B

Starboard side, compartment #1.   B

Galley.   B

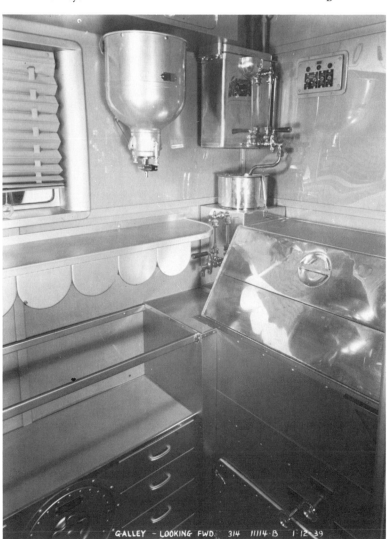

Cutaway of the prototype of the Boeing 314.

B

Access to the engines was available both for inflight service and ground repairs.
GW

Planes were berthed at Mathews Beach on Lake Washington until they were turned over to Pan Am. GW

The prototype B-314 on a test run on Lake Washington in Seattle. B

Three-quarter front view, April 1939.

GW

Moonlight at Mathews
Beach.　GW

Polishing the props.   GW

Nose, port side, July 1941.
                         B

The B-314 had one problem as this photo amply demonstrates. The fuselage-mounted sponsons, in a strong crosswind, could cause the wing tip to drag the water. Wing-mounted sponsons might have prevented this, but would have produced other problems. This photo is of an early model with a single tail.   GW

The two famous Pan Am Clippers, M-130 (left) and B-314, off Treasure Island, San Francisco Bay, 1939.   GW

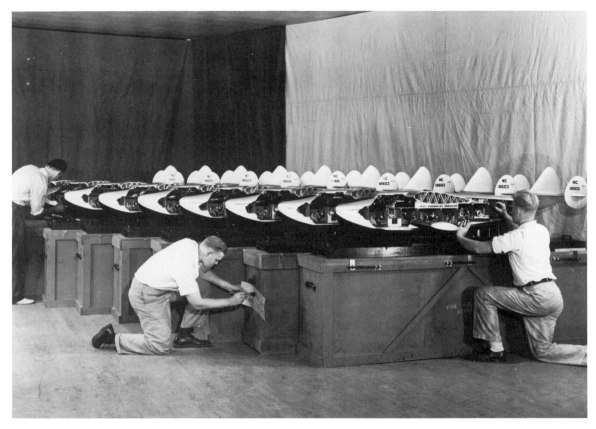

Workers put the finishing touches on B-314 models at the Boeing factory for distribution to Pan Am ticket offices around the world.   B

Edmund T. Allen (left), Boeing test pilot, and Capt. Harold Gray, senior pilot for Pan Am inspect the Clipper's stainless steel anchor on the dock at Plant #1.   B

Passengers deplaning at Treasure Island. B

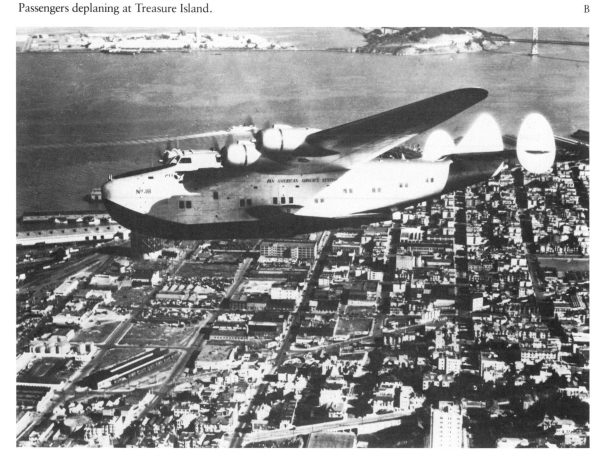

A Clipper over San Francisco. B

III. BEACHING

When preparing to beach the airplane, the gear should be attached to the hull while both are afloat. The following procedure is suggested, assuming that the airplane is to be beached bow first.

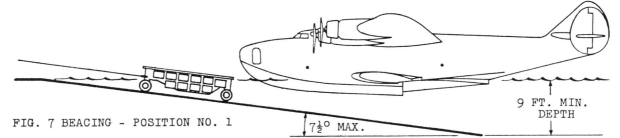

FIG. 7 BEACING - POSITION NO. 1 $7\frac{1}{2}°$ MAX.

9 FT. MIN. DEPTH

In Figure 7, the corner drums have been sufficiently filled before entering the water to cause the gear to float with the upper structure awash.

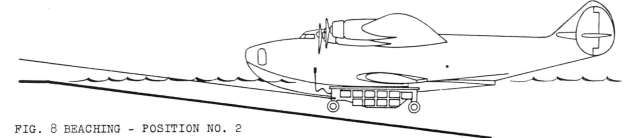

FIG. 8 BEACHING - POSITION NO. 2

Figure 8 shows the gear afloat and bearing up slightly on the hull bottom. As the gear is pulled back along the hull, the forward positioning cables should be placed into their sockets in the hull to prevent the gear from rolling too far aft. Do not allow the wheels to touch the ramp until it is properly positioned, as any movement of the water may cause the airplane to settle on the gear in the wrong position and thus damage the hull. The exact position of the gear on the hull can be determined when the step drops over the rear rollers of the beaching gear, as shown in Figure 9.

CAUTION: THE CRADLES MUST BEAR ON THE BULKHEADS BEFORE ALLOWING THE GEAR TO TOUCH THE RAMP.

Miscellaneous notes on design, performance, ect., taken by W.E. Beall during Boeing Model 314 shakedown flight from San Francisco to Hong Kong, China and return. February 1939.

PAA

ALAMEDA

With assurances that Pan Am would have a mail contract across the Pacific as well as the use of Midway, Wake and Guam as stopping points, the airline built bases for its proposed service. William Grooch, operations manager of CNAC (China National Aviation Corporation), was called back from China to head the construction crew. Grooch leased property on the north shore of Alameda, directly across the bay from San Francisco, as a site for Pan Am's West Coast terminal.

A yacht basin already existed at Alameda, and additional facilities were constructed to handle the large flying boats. Although the Alameda base served the Clippers for five years, it was intended to be a temporary facility as the Navy for many years had planned to build its own base at Alameda. Thus, on Jan. 23, 1939, Pan Am moved its entire operation from Alameda to Treasure Island in San Francisco Bay. Pan Am's Alameda base no longer exists, and the site is now occupied by the Naval Air Station Alameda.

Maintenance crew at the Alameda base, December 1936.   SS

A crowd gathers at the Alameda airport on Nov. 11, 1935, to greet the M-130 *China Clipper* upon its arrival from the Baltimore factory.   PAA

A crowd gathered at Alameda to send off another Clipper across the Pacific.   PAA

Hawaii Clipper at Alameda, October 1936.   SS

The *Hawaii Clipper* on its cradle, running up its engines before entering the water. October 1936.   SS

In California, the Clippers were serviced by extensive repair facilities. As pictured here, the facility could make overhauls or complete engine changes.   PAA

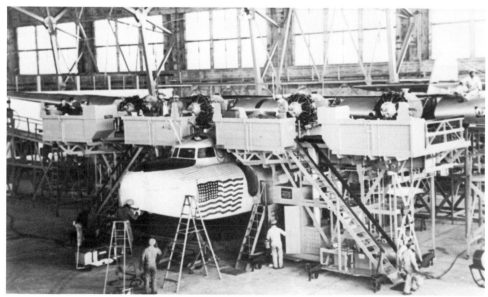

TREASURE ISLAND

A man-made island, Treasure Island was built as the site of the 1939 Golden Gate International Exposition and as a municipal airport for the San Francisco Bay area. The island-building project was undertaken by the U.S. Army Corps of Engineers at a cost of about $4 million and was funded by the WPA (Works Progress Administration). Pan Am would occupy a site on the island both during and after the exposition.

The 40-acre island is about a mile long and two-thirds of a mile wide and sits about 13 feet above sea level. Its soil was dredged up from the harbor floor. Lying just north of Yerba Buena Island in San Fran-

cisco Bay, Treasure Island is connected by causeway with the San Francisco-Oakland Bay Bridge, which opened in 1936.

Of the 14 possible sites that were examined in the Bay area for a land-seaplane port, Treasure Island was the best. It allowed takeoffs and landings in a 270-degree radius, and had good prevailing winds and approach zones that were clear of obstructions. Air density conditions were near-perfect with cool line air ensured by the surrounding water, while light, steady breezes permitted a long, low approach over the Oakland tideflats. Fog was not considered much of a problem in this part of the Bay.

Three permanent buildings—a main terminal and two hangars—were constructed on Treasure Island for use by Pan American and other airlines. The main terminal was built with a dual purpose—during the exposition, it served as an administration building for the festivities and later it would serve as an airline terminal. A huge semicircle of concrete, it is three stories high and measures 380 feet across.

The 220-foot-long passenger concourse occupied the main floor of the terminal, while upper floors and wings of the building housed restaurants, dormitories, offices, a weather station, and public observation galleries. Facilities for freight, mail, and customer services were located in the basement, which also provided access to five ramps used to load seaplanes as well as regular aircraft. The building was topped by

Treasure Island is a man-made island in San Francisco Bay. It was created for the fair and later used as an airport. In the right background is San Francisco and the San Francisco-Oakland Bay Bridge.

Naval/Marine Corps Museum, Treasure Island

An artist's rendering of the proposed Pan Am terminal and hangar that would be built on Treasure Island in San Francisco Bay for the 1939 Golden Gate International Exposition. The terminal building would be used as the fair's administrative offices and then turned over to airline use.   Naval/Marine Corps Museum, Treasure Island

Pan Am's display for the exposition was located inside the Hall of Airline Transportation hangar. 1939-40.
Naval/Marine Corps Museum, Treasure Island

the airport control tower.

The two hangars, built of steel and concrete and over 300 feet long, were used for storage and maintenance. Like the main terminal, they hugged the south seawall of Treasure Island and thus left the rest of the island free for runways.

As a mooring basin, the Clippers used Treasure Cove, the area between Treasure and Yerba Buena islands, which was bordered by the causeways. About a quarter-mile wide and two-thirds of a mile long, this basin was served by a beaching ramp and marine railway for hauling Clippers into the hangar, loading docks for passengers and freight, a refueling dock, and mooring buoys and walkways.

Pan Am used Treasure Island as its first permanent base and was also an exhibitor at the fair, being the exposition's first tenant and one of its prime attractions. The exhibition showed the inner workings of the world's largest transoceanic airline. As part of the Pan Am exhibition, seen by more than 2.5 million visitors, plate-glass windows were installed in one of Treasure Island's hangars, known as the Hall of Air Transportation. The exhibition area in the hangar could house two Clippers, and one of the flying boats was kept on display at all times. Visitors could watch the complete overhaul of the world's largest commercial aircraft, as well as the etching of propellers and the checking of instruments.

Not long after Pan Am moved to Treasure Island, war broke out in Europe, and Japan was threatening in the Pacific. Then came the Pearl Harbor attack, and plans for a civilian airport at Treasure Island were shelved. Soon Pan Am was sharing the airport facilities with the Navy.

By 1944, the Navy's facilities on the island had become so large that Pan Am was forced to move to the new San Francisco Airport (Mills Field), located south of the city and now the site of San Francisco International Airport. Flying-boat service was suspended shortly after the end of the war.

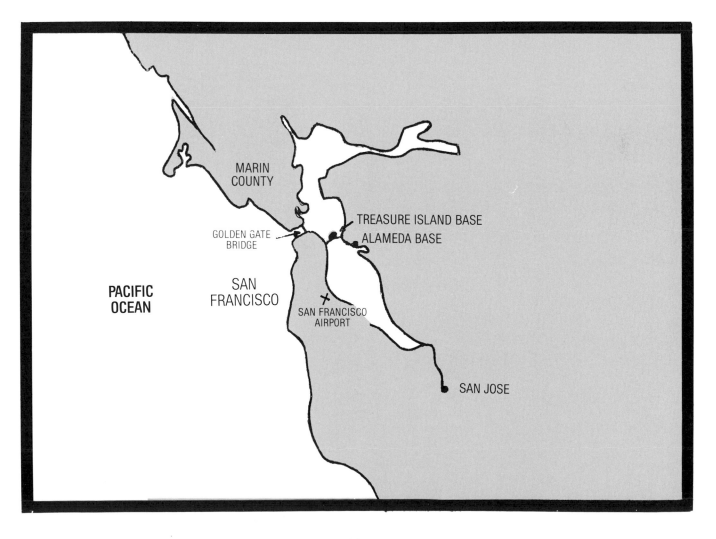

Aerial view of the Golden Gate International Exposition, held on Treasure Island in 1939 and 1940. The large building in the right foreground served as Pan Am's Clipper base while the fair was in progress. When the fair closed in 1940, the large building in the left foreground was taken over for Pan Am's terminal.   PAA

The *Philippine Clipper* moored at Treasure Island with Yerba Buena Island in the background.　PAA

Passengers ready to board a Clipper at Alameda.　PAA

Passengers and crew preparing to board a Clipper. The large crowd in the background was made up of fairgoers. The big hangar behind them was built for Pan Am by the fair and is still in existence.　PAA

A B-314 moored at Treasure Island. This photo was probably taken in early 1939, as it appears construction is still under way for the Golden Gate International Exposition.
PAA

The *China Clipper* beached at Treasure Island with the Oakland Bay Bridge in the background.   PAA

A Pan American globe used in the 1930s is now on display at the Navy/Marine Corps Museum at Treasure Island.

Pan Am's famous globe, which was on display at the airline's fair exhibit.   Naval/Marine Corps Museum, Treasure Island

Today the only major remains of the fair are the administrative building/Pan Am terminal (top) and two original hangars (bottom). The terminal building now houses Navy offices and a Navy/Marine Corps museum. Treasure Island itself currently is a Navy base.

A ground attendant with passengers at Treasure Island.
PAA

The *Philippine Clipper* flying over Alcatraz Prison in San Francisco Bay.   PAA

Flying over San Francisco Bay.   PAA

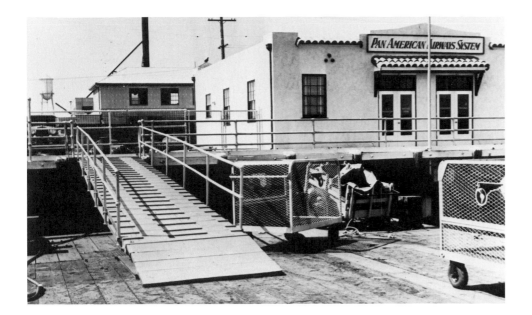

In 1939, a Clipper base was established in Los Angeles.
PAA

By 1945, the Clippers were using the new San Francisco Airport, located south of the city. With the end of the war, however, the flying boats were obsolete. An era had ended.   GW

The Pearl City base.   NA

CHAPTER SEVEN

THE HAWAII BASE

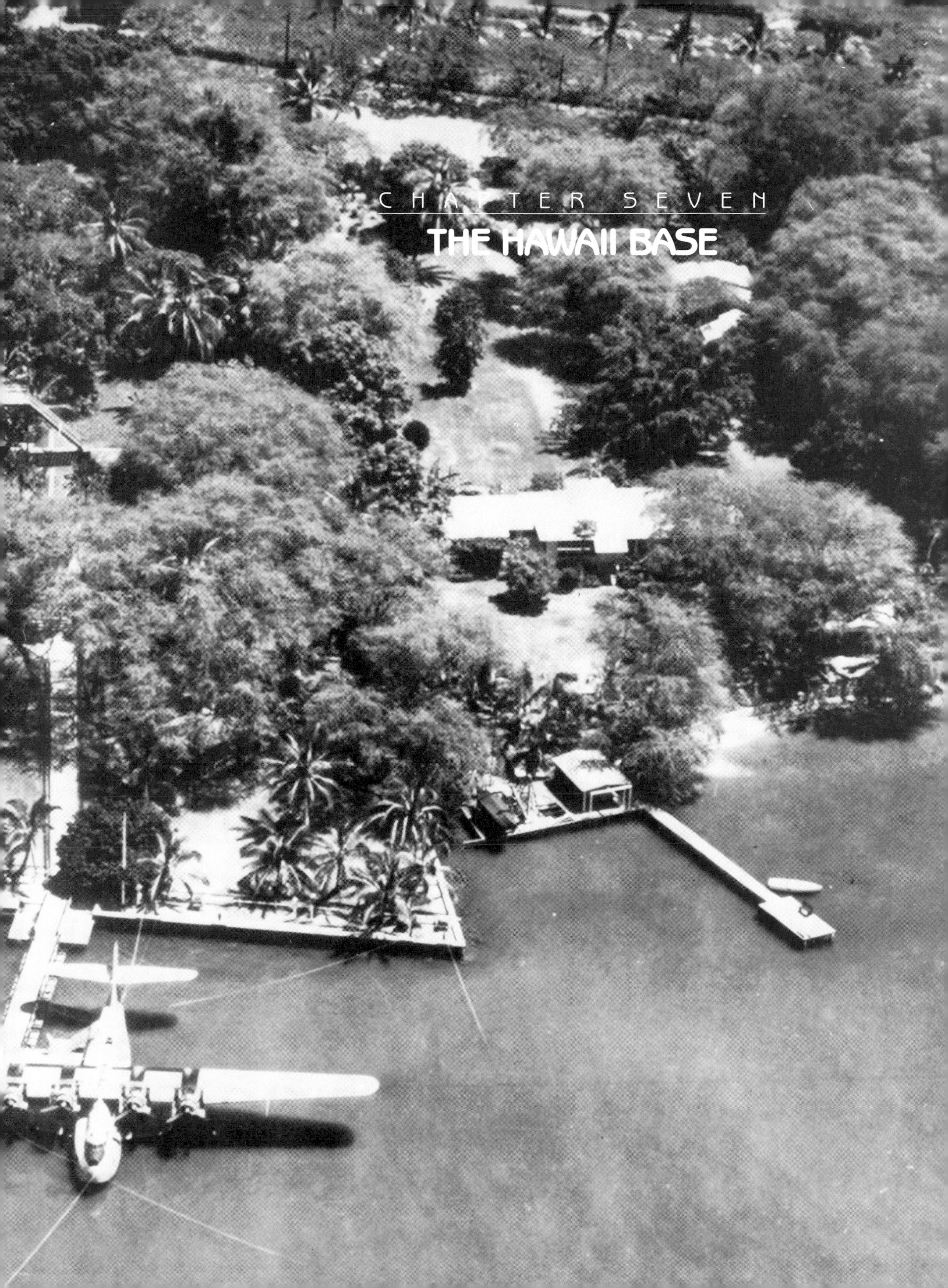

A seaplane base had been in existence for many years at the Ford Island Naval Air Station at Pearl Harbor, 10 miles from Honolulu. The first survey flights in 1935 used this facility but Pan Am was in need of a permanent base in the harbor area. After the long flight from San Francisco, the M-130 Clipper would need to lay over for refueling, resupply and rest. The crew and passengers (when this service started in 1936) were usually taken to the Royal Hawaiian Hotel on Waikiki for their overnight stay.

A site was purchased on the Pearl City Peninsula op-posite the Middle Loch of Pearl Harbor for a permanent clipper base. It was opened in 1935 and the first airmail flight landed there on November 22. The new facilities serviced passengers and freight and provided for the maintenance and repair of the flying boats until Clipper flights were discontinued in 1946.

Through the years the base was expanded and the site is now part of the Navy's housing area. Today all of the buildings are gone but several of the concrete pads and a short dock still remain.

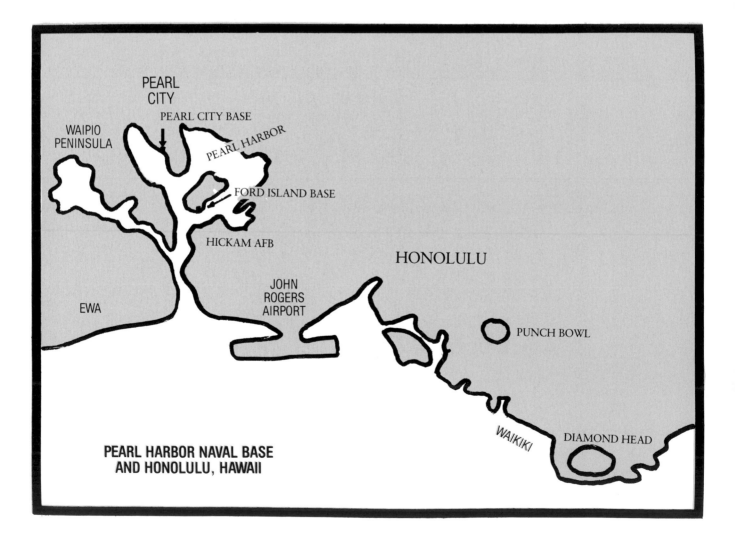

PEARL HARBOR NAVAL BASE AND HONOLULU, HAWAII

A Clipper lifts off from the waters near Ford Island on her way to San Francisco.   HA

The S-42 *Hong Kong Clipper* at Pearl Harbor on Dec. 15, 1937. Notice the curious spectator swimming alongside.   NA

Stations at Midway and Wake depended on supplies from Honolulu, including a weekly supply of library books flown in from the Honolulu Public Library. Librarians Laura Sutherland, left, and Margaret Newland hand books to PAA employee J.A. Brooks. HA

An RCA Victor radio set arrives at Honolulu in 1937. On the left is W.D. Stone, merchandising manager for Mutual Telephone Co., RCA's distributor. On the right is J.A. Brooks, a PAA employee. HA

Mrs. Mary Kearny receives the largest postcard ever delivered by air. The twenty-hour flight from California to Honolulu required $10.50 in postage for a card this size. HA

Flying businessmen arrive in Hawaii via Clipper. From left: Wallace Alexander, chairman of the board, Alexander and Baldwin; Paul Patterson, publisher of the *Baltimore Sun;* Cornelius N. Whitney, chairman of Pan Am's board of directors; Roy Howard, chairman of the Scripps-Howard newspapers; William Roth, chairman and president of the Matson Steamship Line; Senator William McAdoo; Amon G. Carter, publisher of the *Fort Worth Star Telegram*, and Juan Trippe. This flight, which was organized by Trippe, himself, took place a week before the initial scheduled passenger flight of Oct. 27, 1936.   HA

This group flew from California to Hawaii in the B-314 *California Clipper* in 1939. The B-314 could make the 2400-mile trip in 15 hours.
HA

One of the oldest passengers, Dr. Alfred L. Arnold (80), and one of the youngest, Susan Brothers (four months), to fly on the *Hawaii Clipper*.
PAA

The Clipper crew is treated to a luau following the Polynesian christening of the *Honolulu Clipper*. At the head of the table is Capt. R.H. McGlohn. Leaning forward with leis is Joseph B. Poindexter, governor of the territory of Hawaii. His daughter, Helen, sits next to him.
HA

Helen Poindexter (left center), daughter of the governor of Hawaii, aids in the christening of the B-314 *Honolulu Clipper* in Hawaii in 1939 after the Clipper's flight from California. HA

In early 1940, Pan Am moved its base to the Pearl City Peninsula, across from Middle Loch. This base served commercial flights until the start of World War II.   HA

Passengers disembark from the *Philippine Clipper* at the Pearl City base.   HA

Pearl City before the arrival of Pan Am, overlooking the Middle Loch of Pearl Harbor.
PAA

A house at the Pearl City base before it was purchased by Pan Am.   PAA

Mail and cargo buildings (left) and the PAA terminal building (right) at Pearl City during the war years.   PAA

Part of the remains of the
Pearl City base in 1984.

The *North Haven* lies off the dock at Wake (Wilkes Islet) on her second trip to the Pacific Islands.   PAA

PAA

NORTH HAVEN

Once Pan Am decided to establish a string of seaplane bases across the Pacific, attention had to be turned to developing facilities for planes and personnel. In Hawaii and the Philippines, Pan Am could make use of established facilities and regular freight shipments. On Guam, an abandoned, U.S. Marine Corps flying-boat base could be taken over and remodeled.

However, on Midway and Wake—vital links in the proposed chain of outposts—there were no facilities. Pan Am would have to start from scratch, transporting all the amenities of life to these islands, from drinking water to topsoil, along with aviation fuel and prefabricated hotels.

The company chartered the 15,000-ton steamer *North Haven* in Seattle and brought it to San Francisco where she would be loaded with a remarkable cargo. One hundred thousand items weighing 6,000 tons were stowed on board. Along with the Pan Am

cargo, the *North Haven* would have to carry enough supplies to sustain a 74-man construction crew, 44 technicians and 32 ship's crewmen for many months.

Her decks and holds loaded with supplies, the *North Haven* shipped out of San Francisco on March 27, 1935. More supplies were taken on at Honolulu, including a ton of dynamite, and more personnel came on board, including Chinese house-boys and a young man named Bill Mullahey. Mullahey, with George Kuhn, would play an important role in the Wake operation, blasting a channel through the coral in the inner lagoon.

Several days out of Honolulu, the *North Haven* anchored off Midway. Because of shallow water, the ship was forced to stay four miles out, which created problems in unloading supplies and equipment. Barges and launches had to contend with rolling, heavy seas. Supplies and heavy equipment had to be swung out and dropped into them. The task did not get any easier once ashore. Supplies had to be man-

On the dock at San Francisco, everything from tractors to toilet paper awaits shipment to the facilities at Midway, Wake and Guam.
PAA

The *North Haven* loads a mooring barge in San Francisco before beginning her historic journey to the Central Pacific on March 27, 1935.

PAA

handled over the reefs and dragged over fine sand by tractors to the construction site. As if to add insult to injury, thousands of Laysan albatross, or Gooney birds, greeted the men of the *North Haven* to Midway. Their nests proved a hazard every step of the way.

Twenty-four of the work force stayed on Midway when the *North. Haven* weighed anchor and set sail for Wake, 1,200 miles further west. Wake was an unknown entity. The small lagoon had been charted in 1923, but as yet it was a gamble as to whether the lagoon could be used to land flying boats safely.

On May 9, 1935, the *North Haven* dropped anchor on the ocean side of Wilkes Islet. Several discouraging discoveries were quickly made. Pan Am had planned to construct its seaplane station on Wilkes Islet, but on-site inspections quickly showed that Peale Islet, across the lagoon from Wilkes, would be the better site. To make matters more difficult, prevailing wind conditions would not allow the *North Haven* to anchor off Peale. And there was no entrance into the lagoon through which barges could ferry supplies from the ship to Peale.

Supplies would have to be off-loaded from the ship, barged to Wilkes, pulled over the sand to the lagoon, and reloaded on barges for the final trip to Peale. In time, a short, homemade railroad would be built, running halfway across Wilkes to the lagoon.

Equally discouraging was the lack of fresh water on Peale. Drilling wells proved to be a futile task. Instead, the careful hoarding of rainwater would be the answer to Wake's water problem.

Slowly, under the supervision of Frank McKenzie, Pan Am's Wake facilities began to take shape. Tents housed construction crews while an airport office, storage buildings, a seaplane ramp, radio antennas and permanent housing were built. On both islands, the work was hard and there was little to do for recreation other than lie in the sun or swim.

On Midway construction crews built a nine-hole golf course of sorts. The men on Midway were somewhat more fortunate than those on Wake, for Midway boasted tennis courts and a baseball field built by the Cable Company personnel. And, of course, there were always Gooney birds for spectators. On both islands, however, the life of a construction worker was a lonely one.

The *North Haven* sailed on to Guam and the Philippines with radio equipment to complete stations there. On her return, she picked up some members of the construction crews from both islands.

On Wake and Midway, the next step would be to build overnight accommodations for future Clipper passengers. Once again the *North Haven* was loaded in San Francisco, this time with complete, prefabri-

cated hotels, everything from stairways to ashtrays, leaving California on Jan. 15, 1936.

Workers constructed identical hotels on Midway and Wake, and refurbished a building at the Guam base. Each hotel had a central lobby, two wings and wide verandas. Each room boasted of a bath, and the hotels were decorated to make the overnight passenger feel as comfortable as possible. Pan Am recruited waiters and cooks from the Chamorros of Guam to staff their hotels.

The following newspaper article, dated Jan. 15, 1936, gives a vivid account of the hotels' construction and accommodations.

PACIFIC AIRLINE SHIPS TWO HOTELS

PREFABRICATED BUILDINGS SENT TO MIDWAY AND WAKE ISLANDS TO CARE FOR PLANE TRAVELERS.

RUSHED TO MEET DEMANDS

REQUESTS FOR TRANSPORT TO FAR EAST LARGER AND EARLIER THAN COMPANY EXPECTED.

Two complete, prefabricated hotels of forty-five rooms each were among the 6,000-ton cargo of the Pan American chartered supply ship North Haven, it was disclosed yesterday, when she sailed from San Francisco on Monday night for the island bases of the airline across the Pacific Ocean. The two hotels will be erected at Midway Island and Wake Island.

It had not been intended to set up passenger facilities so soon, officials of the airline said yesterday, nor had so much interest as has been developed in the island bases themselves been anticipated. Demand for passenger service, following the mail flights, has been so great however, they explained, that the whole program has been advanced by many months, and stop-over facilities on Midway and Wake are now expected to be available by May 15, when the North Haven is due to return to California.

The prefabricated hotels, of frame construction, are complete in all details, including furnishings. Designed for the special conditions on tropical islands, they consist of two wings built with a central, circular lobby. They have wide verandas. Each room has a shower bath with hot water.

Full furniture for the social rooms and bedrooms, down to coat hangers and ash trays, is in the vessel's cargo, as well as cashier's cages, desks, draperies, inter-room telephones and scores of other items.

The North Haven also carries materials for building aquaria, as it is believed that visitors will be interested in the brilliantly colored fish of the island.

The North Haven also carries 250,000 gallons of gasoline for the bases, six months' supplies of groceries and canned foods, lighting equipment and a sand sledge for transferring passengers from the mooring dock to the base at Midway, a distance of about a quarter of a mile. The sand, it was explained, is so soft that road building is difficult.

Additional Chinese servants for the Midway and Wake bases will be shipped at Honolulu, and certain passenger facilities for installation at Macao, the Portuguese settlement on the Chinese coast which will be the Eastern terminus of the line, will be carried as far as Manila and there transshipped.

The supply expedition is in charge of Frank McKenzie, who has been shipped as supercargo on the North Haven. He has under him a construction crew of eighty-six men.

One year and nine months after the first *North Haven* expedition had left San Francisco, Pan Am was ready to bring passengers aboard its Clipper flights. Mail flights had been stopping at the islands since November of 1935. On Oct. 21, 1936, passenger service began.

MIDWAY

Midway Island, first stop for Clippers flying west from Hawaii, lies 1,380 miles northwest of Oahu. Actually two islands, Sand and Eastern, Midway has the distinction of being the oldest territory of the United States, claimed by Capt. N.C. Middlebrooks on July 5, 1859. On first discovery, this speck of land (Sand Island) one and a half miles from any neighbor at Lat. 20° 13' North, Long. 177° 22' West, was named Brooks Island. In 1867, the USS *Lackawanna* visited the coral atoll, hoisting the American flag and giving the island group the name of Midway, noting that these islands are halfway round the world from the Greenwich, England meridian.

Midway's annexation aroused considerable interest in the United States. A proposal was made that Midway be developed as a coaling station, a proposal opposed by Honolulu businessmen who saw no reason to encourage competition. Other interests in Hawaii feared that the development of Midway might reduce the chances of Hawaii's annexation by the United States. Congress, however, appropriated $50,000 to blast a channel through the reef and dredge a harbor.

When the *USS Saginaw*, assigned to carry out the will of Congress, arrived at Midway, her work was hampered by gales and the project was temporarily postponed. On her way back to Honolulu, the *Saginaw* piled up on the rocks off of Ocean Island. The loss of the ship, along with the original opposition to the plan, led to the abandonment of efforts to develop Midway.

At the turn of the century, Midway once again came to the attention of the public. Two crews were laying the first trans-Pacific cable, one working west from Hawaii, the other working east from Guam. They met on Midway in June of 1903. With the establishment of the island as a relay station, permanent residents came to Midway for the first time. The civilian force was joined briefly by a U.S. Marine garrison until, following the explosion of the ammunition dump, the military post was abandoned.

With the growing military importance of seapower following World War I, the United States gave thought to fortifying Midway. The Washington Naval Treaty of

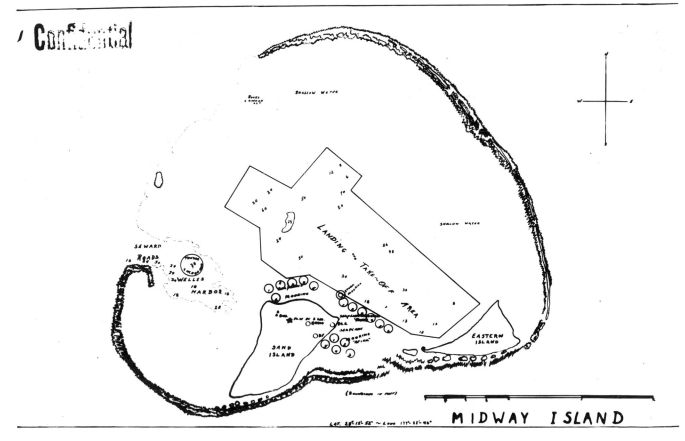

Landing area in the lagoon at Midway.

PAA

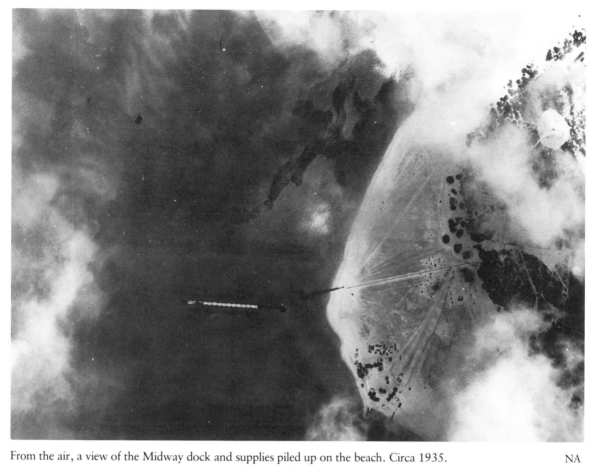

From the air, a view of the Midway dock and supplies piled up on the beach. Circa 1935.   NA

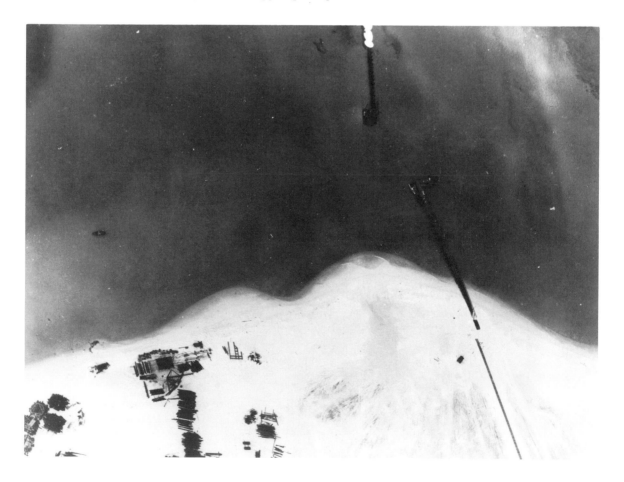

Unloading supplies at Midway (Sand Island) in 1935.
PAA

SUPPLIES FROM SS NORTH HAVEN WERE MATERIAL HAD TO BARGED IN, DUE NO CHANNELS

The dock at Midway.   PAA

1921–22, however, prohibited the fortification of these islands. The treaty permitted commercial enterprises, and Midway continued to be used as a cable station.

In 1935, Pan Am came to Midway, bringing 100 tons of topsoil from Guam aboard the *North Haven*, only to have the Navy refuse to allow the topsoil to be unloaded until a certificate of purity could be produced. Pan Am's Midway station manager, J. Parker Van-Zandt, managed to satisfy the Navy by flying in a certificate from Guam, signed by Guam's plant and animal inspector. This would not be the last time Pan Am would have to deal with fears of contamination. In 1936, the fumigation of commercial aircraft departing Midway for Hawaii was initiated to ward off the introduction of insects that might prove harmful to Hawaiian agriculture.

Although a part of the Hawaiian chain of islands, Midway, unlike her nearest neighbor, Kure, did not become a part of the state of Hawaii. Today the island of Midway is administered as a territory of the United States by the U.S. Navy. The Naval Air Facility is maintained in a caretaker status, and both island and facility are overseen by a civilian contractor. A 10-man U.S. Navy team is present on the island to monitor the contract.

Nothing remains of Pan Am's Clipper base. However, the original Cable Company buildings, which were used at one time by the airline, are still standing. Constructed around 1906, they are listed on the National Registrar of Historic Places.

The Gooney birds, of course, still reside on Midway. Numbering over 200,000, they can be seen on every part of the island.

The first laundry for PAA personnel was a 55-gallon drum, powered by elbow grease.
PAA

The first airport office, a wall tent. PAA

Fuel stocks on Sand Island.
PAA

The famous gooney birds of
Midway.   PAA

With the establishment of the
hotel, laundry facilities improved.   PAA

MIDWAY IS READY AS PACIFIC AIRPORT

All Major Construction on the Island Completed 15 Days Ahead of Schedule.

LATEST AMERICAN COLONY

The Community in Mid-Ocean Now Awaits Arrival of First Plane on Route.

1935

By KARL F. LEUDER.

Special Cable to THE NEW YORK TIMES.

MIDWAY ISLANDS, June 6.— This tiny dot on the map of the Pacific—nearly 1,400 miles from the nearest civilization—has now become the newest colony under the Stars and Stripes and is the world's first mid-ocean air base. All of the major construction was completed today, and all the equipment and facilities were pronounced ready to receive the first flying Clipper ships that will pioneer an aerial trade route between California and the Orient.

This island, Sand Island, the largest of the three atolls composing the Midway group, was, except for the cable relay station compound, a virgin jungle forty-five days ago, when the first Pan American Airways pioneers passed over the treacherous shoals from the open sea to take possession of a scrub-matted, coral-strewn area. In those forty-five days a practical miracle has been accomplished.

About 2,000 tons, totaling more than 300,000 items, some weighing as much as 20,000 pounds each, were transferred from the supply ship North Haven to barges, then taken through the dangerous reefs into the lagoon and finally to the beach.

The construction and airways crews, totaling 150 men, labored from dawn often until far into night, unsheltered in the early stages from the blazing sun or tropic downpours. The foundations for buildings were laid and heavy construction completed before the North Haven moved on to Wake Island, leaving a construction crew of twenty-eight and twelve members composing the permanent staff.

The workers are now completing the last stages of plumbing and permanent installation of electric lighting and are painting the buildings. The men will be ready to depart when the North Haven stops to pick them up probably in a month or more after her mission westward to the Philippines. The work is actually fifteen days ahead of the schedule set for the project.

For thirty days the Meteorological Bureau here has been filing daily reports, to which are now added studies of the air up to 35,000 feet. Intensive study of the peculiarities of this section of the Pacific is enabling the meteorologist to forecast the local weather with a high degree of accuracy.

The radio transmitting and receiving stations are maintaining hourly communication schedules with Pan American ground radio control stations both in Hawaii and California. A fourth station in the Pan American Airways' Pacific radio circuit has been added at Wake Island.

The Midway mooring barge.   PAA

One of the small boats that occasionally carried passengers and cargo to and from the clippers.   PAA

Clipper passengers had a long walk to shore from the Midway dock. Station wagons served as taxis.   PAA

The *Philippine Clipper* docked at Midway's mooring barge.   PAA

Passengers embark on the *Hawaii Clipper* at Midway.   PAA

Top left: The Midway beacon, 1937.   PAA

Top right: The Clippers carried some unusual cargo in their 10-year history, including gooney birds from Midway to a new home at San Francisco's Fleischhaker Zoo. A considerable amount of persuasion was necessary to gain permission to ship a few birds from the island.   PAA

Bottom: Pan Am employees on the Midway dock.   PAA

The Pan Am hotel on Midway. A similar hotel was built on Wake.

PAA

The Midway hotel dining room.

The *Midway*, stationed at the island, was used to transfer passengers and freight and occasionally served as a tow boat for the clippers.   PAA

Golfing on Midway Island

For a quiet diversion from the daily routine, PAA personnel golf along the sand with the gooney birds as spectators.
PAA

PAA personnel display the wing span of a gooney bird.
PAA

Cable station buildings on Midway, constructed in 1906 and used in the 1930s as temporary offices and housing for the Pan Am clipper base. They are now listed on the National Register of Historic Places.

Monument to the Battle of Midway.

WAKE

For most of its history, Wake Island was just another speck of coral in the Pacific Ocean. Lying at 19° 18' 40" north latitude and 166° 35' 20" east longitude, Wake is situated 2,600 miles west of Hawaii and 1,500 miles east of Guam. Like Midway, Wake is actually a set of islets: Wake, Wilkes and Peale. The top of a submerged volcano, this atoll has a land mass three square miles and a circumference of about 10 miles. The atoll is ringed by a reef that encloses an inner lagoon. The three islets are separated by Peale and Wilkes channels, two narrow channels that caused considerable problems for inter-islet movement until a causeway was built between Wake and Peale islets.

Wake was discovered in 1586 by the Spanish explorer Alvaro de Mondana, who named the island San Francisco. Covered with a dense undergrowth of shrubs and small trees, with wildlife limited to birds and rats, the atoll was ignored for years.

The islands' second visitor, the British schooner *Prince William Henry*, was commanded by William Wake, who gave his name to the atoll. Yet finding his discovery without water or significant vegetation, he didn't bother to claim it for his king.

The first American visit to the island took place in late 1840, when a flotilla of warships arrived under the command of Commodore Charles Wilkes. But it was not until the Spanish-American War sent a stream of traffic past the island near the turn of the century that anyone bothered to claim Wake. The United States claimed Wake as an American possession on July 4, 1898.

The following year, Cmdr. Edward D. Taussig of the USS *Bennington* raised the American flag over the atoll and established a brass marker, again laying claim to the island for the United States. Between Taussig's expedition in 1899, and Pan Am's decision to build an outpost on the island in 1935, Wake lay in obscurity, visited by an occasional Japanese fishing vessel or westbound U.S. ship.

In 1923, the USS *Tanager* brought a scientific expedition to the island jointly sponsored by Yale University and the Bishop Museum of Honolulu. During their two-week stay, members of the expedition conducted a variety of surveys and formally named one islet for Commodore Wilkes and another for Tilian Peale, the naturalist on the Wilkes expedition.

Like Midway, Wake today is a U.S. territory. Wake

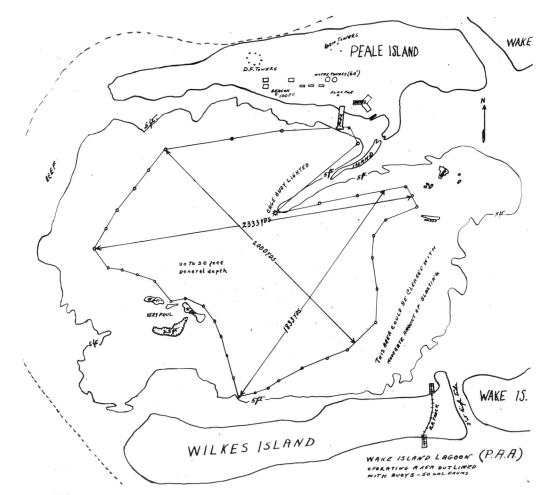

The landing area in Wake's lagoon, as of Nov. 25, 1936.

NA

also serves as a sub-base of the 15th Air Base Wing, Hickam AFB, Hawaii.

Neither man nor weather has been kind to Wake. Typhoons have altered the outline of all three islets. And the constant bombing, first by Japanese and then by American planes, has taken a toll. Yet the fact that the island was once a Pan Am seaplane base is far more evident here than on Midway. Part of the original dock, the seaplane ramp, hotel swimming pool and some concrete pads can still be found on Peale Islet. The remains of facilities constructed during more than three years of Japanese occupation are also much in evidence.

This rare photo shows the unloading area on Wilkes Islet with a small motor launch. From here supplies were taken across the islet on a small railroad track and then transported across the lagoon to Peale Island.   NA

Supplies were ferried by barge to the beach at Wilkes from the *North Haven*.   PAA

A tractor drags supplies over the rocky beach to the railroad tracks.   NA

Eventually, the rails were laid out to the unloading ramp, allowing dockworkers to make use of a small locomotive. Hundreds of 55-gallon drums of diesel fuel and aviation gasoline had to be unloaded by hand. The *North Haven* lies in the background in the lower photo.　　PAA

A temporary rail line was laid across Wilkes to the inner lagoon to facilitate the movement of supplies.　　PAA

Fifty-five-gallon drums are unloaded onto a barge for transport to Wilkes. The drums contained fuel for the diesel generators on the island as well as for the clippers. PAA

A 1935 party held by Wake PAA employees.   PAA

Construction workers lived in these tents on Wilkes before permanent buildings were built on Peale.   NA

After the second supply mission by the *North Haven* in 1936 Wake was transformed into a comfortable overnight stop, with a three-wing hotel, streets, a water system and the facilities needed to service the Clippers.   NA

Another view of the Wake facilities. The direction finder can be seen in the right background.

PAA

The hotel (still under construction) and airport manager's quarters in early 1936. PAA

Airport office just after construction in May of 1935.

NA

This hotel and a similar one on Midway were prefabricated in the United States and shipped on the *North Haven* in January of 1936. It offered all the amenities of any small town hotel including hot and cold running water and a shower in every room.

PAA

A large fountain was constructed in front of the hotel.   PAA

Interior views of the hotel. The dining room featured table cloths and china. Many of the staff were Chamorros from Guam. The rooms were furnished in a style typical of the time.   PAA

A U.S. Army Air Force aerial photo of Peale Island, Oct. 7, 1943, showing remains of the Pan Am facilities in the center.
PAA

The beacon on Wake, used for night landings.   PAA

"Main Street" is casual at the PAA complex on Peale Islet, 1937.

PAA

This Navy photo, taken May 25, 1941, shows the PAA facilities on Peale Islet. The causeway to Wake Islet lies in the lower center. A clipper is tied up to the loading dock, while seven Navy PBYs lie in the lagoon. The *Philippine Clipper* was tied to this dock when strafed on Dec. 8, 1941.
NA

The Wake dock in the 1930s.
PAA

The *Hawaii Clipper* docks at Wake.   PAA

Passengers descend the gangway from the Wake dock to board a Clipper.   PAA

HYDROPONIC GARDENING

Pan Am was ahead of its time in more ways than one. In the late 1930s Pan Am's gardener undertook an unusual experiment in order to provide fresh produce to airline personnel and passengers stopping at Wake on lay-over. The *New York Times*, on Nov. 26, 1939, carried the following account of the airline's efforts to raise vegetables without soil:

Torrey Lyons, chief gardener for Pan American Airways at its Mid-Pacific base at Wake Island, announces that the capacity of his water-culture gardens, in which fresh vegetables are scientifically nurtured, will shortly be quadrupled.

Previously four redwood tanks of 280 square-foot total area yielded average weekly crops of 12 pounds of tomatoes, 8 pounds of cucumbers and experimental lots of lima beans. Raised by hydroponics—the feeding of plants with weak solutions of mineral salts and without earth—the truck crops were used to supplement food supplies shipped to the barren island.

With the addition of a new 70-foot hydroponicum of 980-square-foot area, Mr. Lyons foresees tomato production rising to 30 pounds weekly and his output of other green foods assuming greater stature in the effort to feed the airline's personnel stationed at Wake.

Hydroponic gardening on Wake in 1938. Soil conditions precluded ordinary gardening.　　　　　PAA

The beach on Peale, with the hotel in the background. Recreational activities, including tennis, fishing and swimming, made an overnight stay enjoyable.　　PAA

The original loading/unloading ramp on Peale.

This seaplane ramp originally thought to have been built by Pan Am is now thought to have been built either by the Japanese during the war or the U.S. Navy after the war. Since there was no beaching gear on Wake there was no need for a ramp to service the Clippers.

Remains of one of two water catchment basins next to the hotel site.

A concrete pad that might have been part of the maintenance facility.

GUAM BASE

In 1898, at the end of the Spanish-American War, the island of Guam was ceded to the United States by Spain. Located in the Mariana Island Group, 1500 miles east of the Philippines and 1500 miles west of Wake, the island is 30 miles long and 10 miles wide at its widest point. Guam is the largest and southernmost island of the Mariana archipelago, and in the 1930s was a lonely outpost surrounded by islands under Japanese mandate.

In 1935, Pan American Airways took possession of what had previously been a U.S. Marine Corps sea-plane base at the village of Sumay on Apra Harbor, some six miles south of the capital city of Agana. Pan Am's Clipper facilities were attacked on Dec. 8, 1941, by Japanese forces, and along with the rest of the island fell into Japanese hands. The U.S. recaptured Guam after a month-long campaign in July and August of 1944.

Today the village of Sumay has all but disappeared. The U.S. Naval Ship Repair Facility marks the site of the former clipper base. A small commemorative marker is the only evidence that Guam was once an important Clipper stopover.

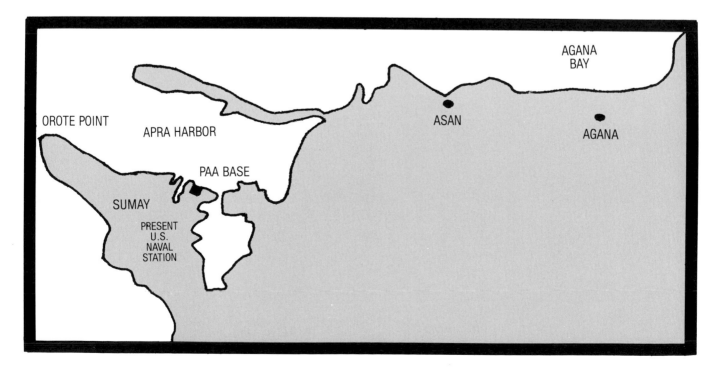

Aerial views of the Pan Am facilities at Sumay and Apra Harbor.

Top: NA
Bottom: PAA

The village of Sumay in the 1930s. The breakwater for the Pan Am base is at the left.   LC

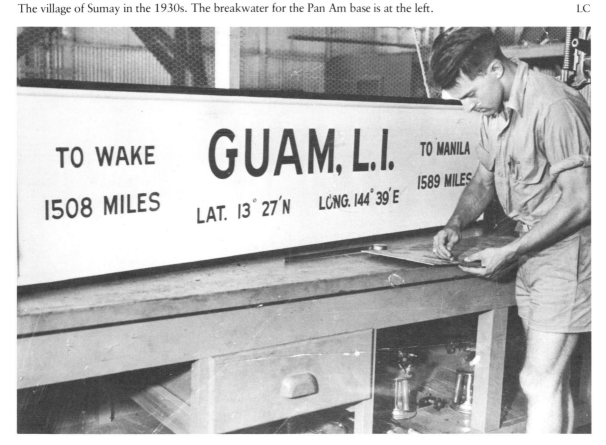

Touching up the entrance sign at Guam's terminal.   PAA

The former flying-boat base of the USMC, Patrol Squadron VP3M, became Pan Am's base at Sumay on Apra Harbor.   PAA

A building near the old Marine Corps base was converted into a hotel for Clipper passengers.   PAA

The dining room served passengers and crew at Sumay.   PAA

Pan Am's facilities at Sumay, 1935. The photo was taken from the top of the 80-foot tower looking out on Apra Harbor. PAA

An addition was added to the hotel in 1941, just months before the hotel was destroyed by Japanese bombers. PAA

The refueling barge at Guam. PAA

Repair facilities were maintained at all stops on the Pacific route. Guam had an extensive stock room (top) and a small parts repair shop (bottom).

PAA

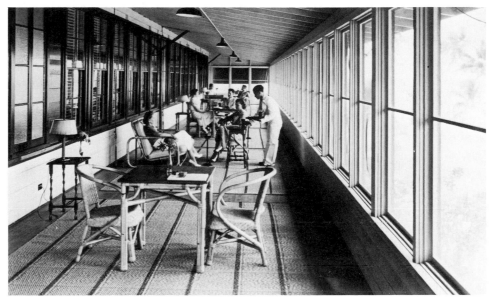

Pan Am's Guam hotel. Top:
The waiting room. Middle:
The veranda.   PAA

The interior of Guam's ticket
office.   PAA

Today there are dry-dock facilities where the Clippers once landed.
Kevin House

Sumay is now part of the U.S. Navy's Ship Repair Facility.
Kevin House

The old Pan Am hotel parking lot is now a go cart track.
Capt. Dale Willoughby

The entrance to Sumay Cove, where the Clippers taxied after landing in the harbor. Capt. Dale Willoughby

Sumay Cove. The Clippers loaded passengers and cargo here.   Kevin House

Marker erected in 1977 marking the approximate site of the Clipper base at Sumay. A 50th anniversary marker was dedicated here on Nov. 24, 1985.

Capt. Dale Willoughby

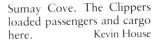

THIS PLAQUE WAS DEDICATED NOVEMBER 24, 1985
BY THE PASSENGERS OF "CHINA CLIPPER II"
DURING CEREMONIES COMMEMORATING THE
50th ANNIVERSARY OF PAN AMERICAN'S
TRANSPACIFIC AIR SERVICE

APRA HARBOR
SUMAY, GUAM
ORIGINAL LANDING SITE OF THE CHINA CLIPPER

A TRIP TO MANILA

Once passenger service began on Oct. 21, 1936, anyone with twelve days and $1600 to spare could fly round trip from the United States to Hong Kong on one of Pan Am's Martin Clippers. For just $720, no small sum in 1936, one could fly to Honolulu and back. Fares of this magnitude were aimed primarily at the business trade during the 1930s, years of the Great Depression.

Passengers would embark on the Clipper at Pan Am's Alameda base in mid-afternoon. After checking the water for dangerous debris, the Clipper's pilot would rev up the plane's engines to full power, accelerating rapidly from 70 to 80 knots for take off. The Clipper would ascend to an altitude of 9,000 feet, where she would cruise at approximately 125 mph. A passenger looking out the window could see the hills of San Francisco and the Golden Gate. He would see nothing but water for the next eighteen hours, until Hawaii came into view.

Long before Hawaii came into sight, dinner would be served on tables covered with linen and fine china. After serving dinner, the stewards would busy themselves preparing the sleeping berths. Clippers left California in the late afternoon in order to land in Hawaii during daylight hours, thus necessitating sleeping accommodations for their much catered-to passengers.

Early the next morning the Clipper would pass over the beautiful island of Molokai, then cross Oahu, landing at the Pearl City base in Pearl Harbor. Passengers continuing west would be taken by car to Waikiki, where they would spend the night in the Royal Hawaiian Hotel.

Early the next morning, the clipper would take off again, this time for Midway, flying over the Oahu landmarks of Ewa and Barber's Point, and then the island of Kauai, the Garden Isle. Several of the smaller islands of the Hawaiian chain—Necker, French Frigate Shoals, Maro Reef, Laysan, Pearl Reef and Hermes Reef—would come into view before a passenger would catch sight of Midway's Sand and Eastern Islets.

Passengers spent the night at the Pan Am hotel on Midway before embarking again in the morning for the 1,200-mile trip to Wake. The time on board might be spent playing cards or catching up on correspondence, for the view on this leg of the journey would consist of nothing but the vast Pacific. On the tiny three-square-mile atoll of Wake, a hotel identical to the one on Midway would provide passengers with a comfortable bed, a number of recreational opportunities and a fine dinner, often the highlight of a passenger's stay on the atolls.

From Wake, another day's trip brought the Clipper's passengers to Guam. In addition to the hotel at the Clipper base, Guam boasted a sizeable local com-

munity. However, few Clipper passengers would have Guam as their final destination. Early the next morning, the clipper would take off for Pan Am's major Far East terminal near Manila. If a passenger planned to continue on to Macao or Hong Kong, he would be taken into downtown Manila for an overnight stay at the Manila Hotel. And the next morning, passengers traveling on to Hong Kong, journey's end, would board either an M-130 or, more likely, the S-42 *Hong Kong Clipper*. (Hong Kong service began in 1937.)

A Clipper passenger, his every need seen to by Pan Am, might never realize how hard airline personnel worked to make his trip possible. On the first leg of the trip, the long, eighteen-hour flight to Hawaii, the nine-man crew would work in shifts through the night. At Ford Island, as at every stop along the way, mechanics would check the plane over carefully as they refueled it. On Midway and Wake, refueling had to be done by hand. Fifty-five-gallon drums were hauled over the sand to the lagoon, then motored out to the plane by launch. At each stop, station managers passed meticulously gathered weather information along to clipper pilots. And, prepared for any eventuality, Pan Am mechanics stood ready at Honolulu, Guam and Manila to make major repairs to any ailing member of Pan Am's fleet of flying boats.

PAA

HAWAII CLIPPER

MENU

FLIGHT No. 135. Hawaii Clipper _____ Aug 15 ___ 1937

Relishes

Beef Broth — Hearts Lettuce Asp Tips

Swiss Steak

New Potatoes — Cut String Beans
Sliced Peaches
Asst Cookies
Cream Cheese & Crackers
Tea · Cocoa — Iced Tea
Coffee
Lemonade ·

FROM _Midway_ ____ TO _Wake_ ____

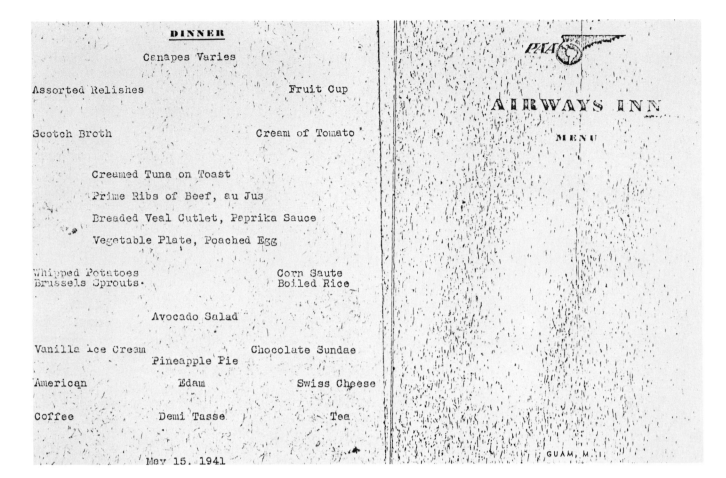

DINNER

Canapes Varies

Assorted Relishes   Fruit Cup

Scotch Broth   Cream of Tomato

Creamed Tuna on Toast

Prime Ribs of Beef, au Jus

Breaded Veal Cutlet, Paprika Sauce

Vegetable Plate, Poached Egg

Whipped Potatoes   Corn Saute
Brussels Sprouts   Boiled Rice

Avocado Salad

Vanilla Ice Cream   Chocolate Sundae
Pineapple Pie

American   Edam   Swiss Cheese

Coffee   Demi Tasse   Tea

May 15, 1941

AIRWAYS INN

MENU

GUAM, M.I.

APERTIFS	GLASS
Dubonnet Imported	$ .30
Sherry Dry or Sweet Imported	.30
Vermouth French or Italian Imported	.30

COCKTAILS	
Bacardi	.35
Clipper	.35
Gibson	.35
Manhattan	.35
Martini Dry or Sweet	.35
Old Fashioned	.35

STILL RED WINES (American)	HALF BOTTLE
Burgundy	$ .50
Claret	.50

STILL WHITE WINES (American)	
Chablis	.50
Sauterne	.50

PORTS AND SHERRIES	GLASS
Old Tawny Imported	$ .30
Spanish Imported	.30
Sherry Imported Dry	.30
Sherry Imported Sweet	.30

CORDIALS AND LIQUEURS	
Benedictine, D.O.M.	.35
Brandy	.35
B and B	.35
Chartreuse, Yellow	.35
Creme De Menthe—Green	.35

LIQUORS—STRAIGHT	
Domestic	GLASS
Bourbon	.30
Rye	.30
Imported	
Scotch	.30
Gin, London Dry	.30
Rum, Puerto Rican	.30

MIXED DRINKS	
Brandy and Soda	.35
Cuba Libre	.35
Gin Rickey	.35
Scotch and Soda	.35
Tom Collins	.35
Rum Collins	.35
Whiskey Hi-Ball	.35

BEERS, ALE AND SOFT DRINKS	
Beers, Etc.	BOTTLE
U. S. Eastern Brands	$ .20
U. S. Western Brands	.15
Far Eastern Brands	.15
Soft Drinks	
Coca-Cola	.10
Ginger Ale	.15
Lime Rickey	.15
Root Beer	.15
Sarsaparilla	.15

ONE AND ONE-HALF OUNCES LIQUOR SERVED
EITHER STRAIGHT OR IN HIGHBALLS

The Cavite Pan American Clipper facilities used a former U.S. Marine Corps flying-boat base. PAA

CHAPTER NINE

THE PHILIPPINES BASE

Due to the location of the Philippines and the good relations between the Philippine and American governments, Manila was a natural stopover for Pan Am's flying boats, and for a number of years served as the main western terminus for the M-130s and B-314s.

In traveling to the Philippines, Pan Am followed in the footsteps of other history-making voyageurs. Magellan "discovered" these islands in 1542, initiating centuries of Spanish influence. Spain annexed the Philippines in 1865, only to lose possession of the islands to the United States following the Spanish-American War in 1898. The U.S. pacified the islands after several years of guerilla warfare by Filipino insurrectionists. In 1935, the Philippines were granted Commonwealth status, and Manuel Quezon took office as the first president of the Commonwealth. Full independence was scheduled to be granted in 1946.

Manila Bay was considered too rough for flying-boat landings. Instead, Pan Am leased the old U.S. Marine Corps flying-boat base at the Cavite Naval Base, some eight miles south of the capital city, Manila. Here at Cavite, several of the buildings were renovated in preparation for their new role as clipper terminals in the Far East. Facilities established here would provide the clippers with their westernmost opportunity for major service and repairs.

Direction finders, radio stations and weather stations were constructed at Laoang, San Fernando and other locations in the islands to guide the planes to Cavite. When passenger service was established, passengers were transported from Cavite to Manila by ferry or by road.

The Cavite Naval Base was heavily bombed during the early days of World War II, and quickly occupied by Japanese forces upon their takeover of the Philippine Islands. After the war, a major U.S. Naval facility was established at Subic Bay, north of Manila, and Cavite was turned over to the Philippine government. Nothing remains today of the original Pan Am facilities at Cavite.

This aerial view of Manila in the 1930s shows the Manila Hotel and inlet in the right foreground and the remains of the old walled city in the background. The hotel was a hub of social activity in pre-World War II Manila.   NA

An aerial view of Cavite Naval Base and the Pan Am facilities . NA

Canacao Bay at Cavite. The Pan Am facilities are shown in the lower left of the photo. NA

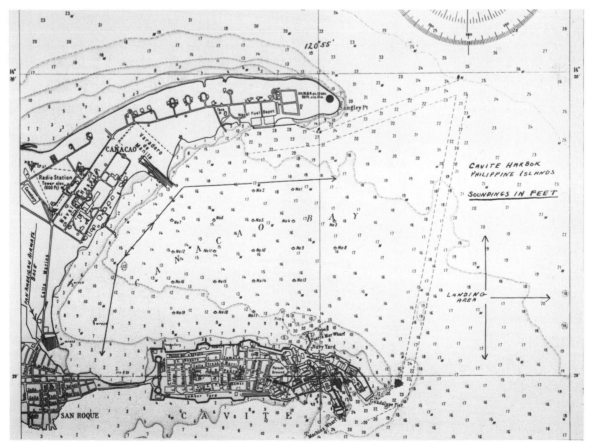

The first B-314 Clipper arrived at Cavite, the Philippines, on March 2, 1939.
PAA

Repair facilities.   PAA

Looking southeast at floating walkway and passenger loading float.   PAA

The temporary base at Cavite. Permanent facilities were under construction at the Navy base. PAA

The terminal building at Cavite, as viewed from the south. Note covered entrance to waiting room on west face of building. PAA

View of dock from passenger platform of terminal building. PAA

The shop, work stands and nose hangar at the Cavite facilities. PAA

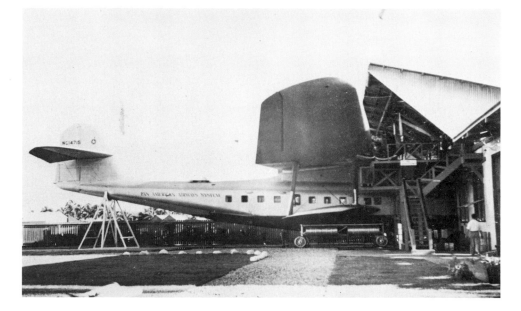

Looking east at dock from porch of terminal building. PAA

The interior of the radio station at Manila, 1937.　　PAA

The direction finder, with its inner and outer systems, guided planes to a safe landing.　　PAA

Radio facilities were established at other locations on the island of Luzon to help guide the planes to Cavite. Left: The D.F. receiver building at San Fernando. Right: The transmitter-receiving building and living quarters at Laoang.　　PAA

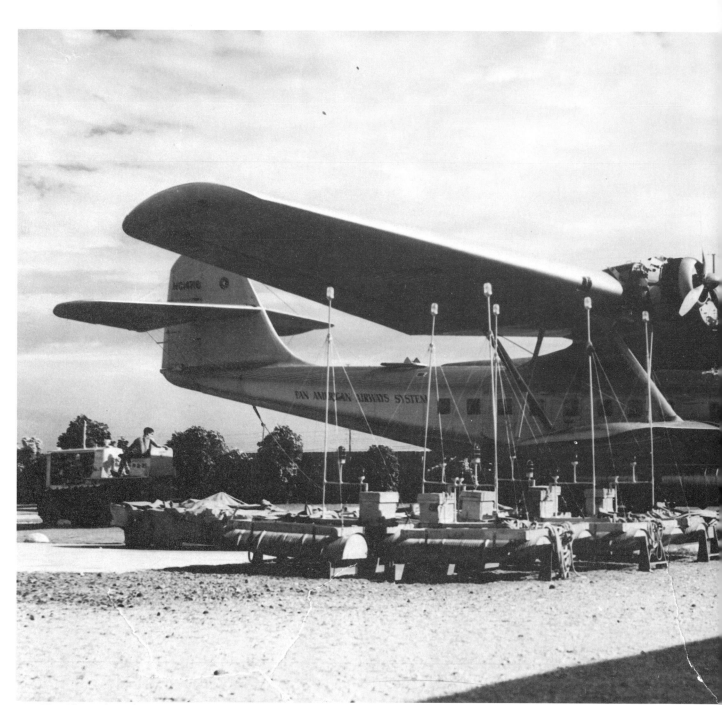

The *China Clipper* being overhauled at the Cavite base. The floats pictured with lights were used for night landings and takeoffs.
Lincoln Hector, Alberton, Mont.

1935 - 1975

At 3:32 in the afternoon of the 29th day of November, 1935, the China Clipper, Pan American World Airways' four-engined flying boat, landed on Manila Bay after spanning 8,000 miles of the Pacific Ocean in 59 hours and 48 minutes from San Francisco, California.

This event marked the first transpacific commercial flight between the United States and the Philippines, and catapulted the young island commonwealth into the world of international aviation.

On this spot, the seven-man crew of the China Clipper, commanded by Captain Edwin Musick, first set foot on Philippine soil.

This marker is dedicated to the intrepid spirit, courage and foresight of American business enterprise that made this historical flight possible, and brought a better understanding between peoples of the Philippines and the United States.

The *China Clipper* at Cavite, 1938.   Lincoln Hector, Alberton, Mont.

A prewar view of the Manila Hotel, social center for Manila.   Manila Hotel

Opposite: The monument erected on the seawall near the Manila Hotel in 1975.   Philippine Airlines

The present-day Manila Hotel with the new annex in the background. The hotel, practically destroyed during the war, has recently been refurbished to its prewar grandeur.   Manila Hotel

An S-42 takes off from Victoria Harbor near Kai-tak Airport.

D-411

CHAPTER TEN

THE HONG KONG/MACAO BASE

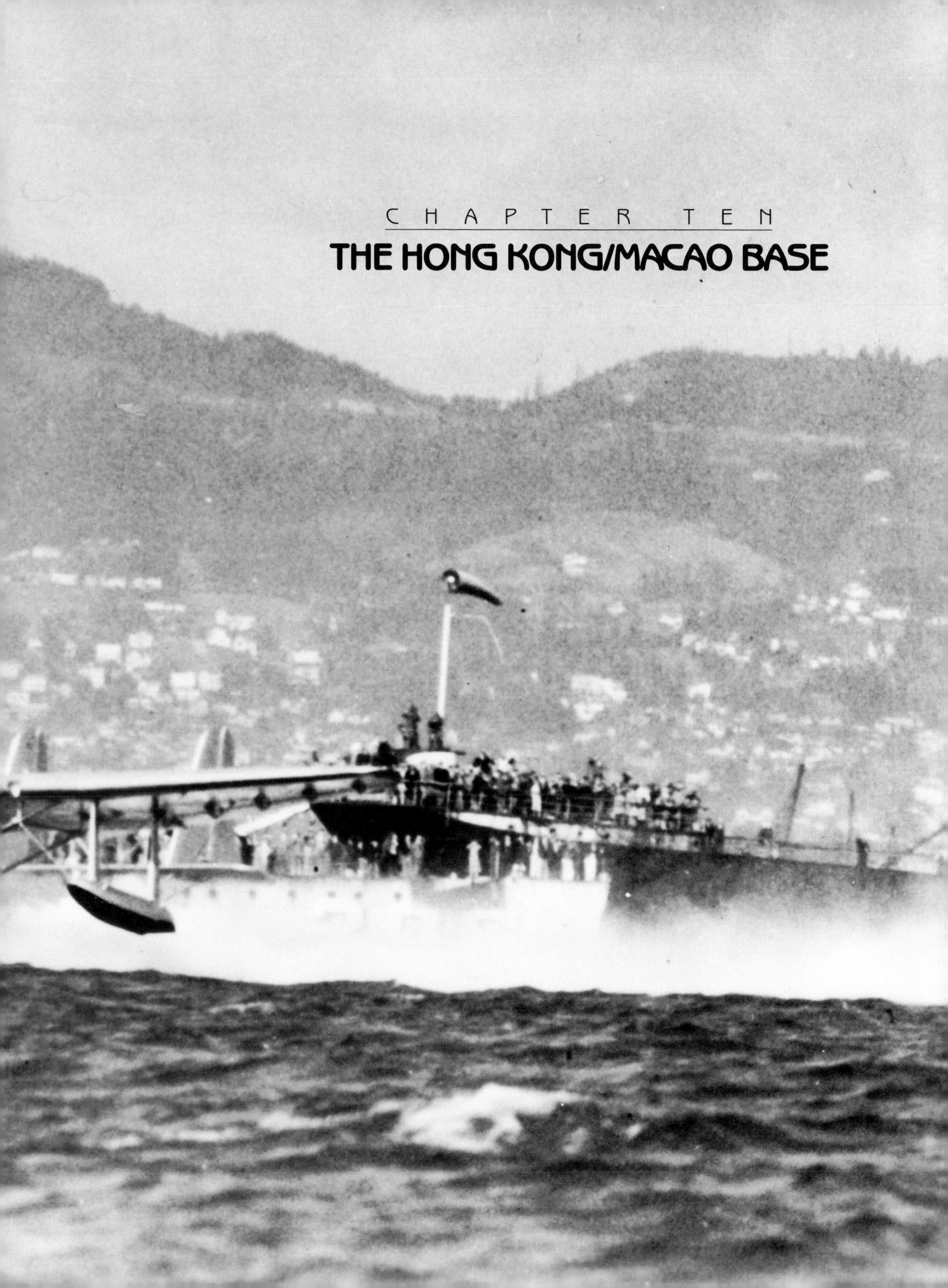

HONG KONG AND MACAO

The base at the eastern end of the Clipper route originally was located at Macao, a Portuguese colony in southeast China. Pan Am had hoped to establish its terminal base at the much larger city of Hong Kong, about 40 miles away, but in 1935, when the airline started mail service from San Francisco to Manila, it could not acquire terminal landing rights at Hong Kong.

Pan Am was particularly eager for a base in Hong Kong, as the city was a terminus for China National Aviation Corporation (CNAC), a Pan Am subsidiary that served the coast and interior of China. But the Clippers' landing rights were denied as the result of actions by British-owned Imperial Airways, which had its eastern terminus at British-governed Hong Kong and which hoped to establish its own trans-Pacific route in the future.

Juan Trippe's strategy in this case was to build the base at Macao and begin operations on the trans-Pacific route in hopes that the British, seeing the success of the service, would offer permission for Pan Am to use Hong Kong as a terminus.

Pan Am's Macao operations included a terminal building, a hangar at the Outer Harbor which was equipped with an office, a radio-telegraph and meteorological station on Macao's Penka Hill, and a planned airstrip that was to be built near the Clipper landing area at the Porto Exterior. The plan was to use the airstrip to transfer passengers and mail to CNAC planes for flights to China. The Clippers were allowed to land briefly at Hong Kong, but could not use the colony as a terminal base.

On Oct. 23, 1936, the *Philippine Clipper* became the first Pan Am passenger and mail flight to Macao (a special flight). It left Manila at 5:45 a.m., alighting at Macao at 10:25 a.m. after circling the city twice. Thousands of citizens turned out to greet the plane, which would stay only briefly before departing to Hong Kong. Among its passengers was Juan Trippe, making an around-the-world flight to check the Pacific route and to explore the possibility of an Atlantic route for the Clippers.

The flight's arrival is described in the following report, filed by a Macao correspondent for Hong Kong's *South China Morning Post*:

"The Outer Port Reclamations of Macao, where the Pan American Airways Company have estab-

lished their station and anchorage, were crowded with an enormous number of persons who turned out to witness the arrival of the Hongkong Clipper from Manila, on the occasion of the inauguration of the Company's regular service from the United States to the China coast.

"The weather was fine, the sky cloudy and slightly overcast, but the visibility was good, and the arrangements for receiving the plane were perfect. The airport station looked trim and business-like, while the grounds were effectively and neatly laid out. The landing stage, consisting of the wharf, with floating pontoons moored close inshore, connected to the wharf by spacious gangways, and terminating in the floating raft, to which the plane was to be moored, were all ready for the plane. . . .

"The Company's staff were in constant touch with the local authorities and for several days before the arrival of the Clipper the Macao Post Office staff was kept busy with mail to be dispatched from Macao. By this morning it was announced that 42,000 covers were to be sent on to Hongkong and other places on the route of the Pan American Services, contained in 10 bags, constituting what was probably a record for the Colony.

"As the hour of the arrival of the Clipper approached, the number of persons and cars at the Station increased, and under Lieut Macedo Pinto, of the Macao Police, the crowd was suitably distributed and there was a respectable orderliness on the part of the enthusiastic multitude. . . .

"Shortly after ten it was announced that the Clipper would soon be in sight, and at 10.15 am it was noticed, flying high over Taipa Island, having been diverted very slightly from the straight line from Manila, probably because of the strong winds prevailing, and after circling over the city of Macao, the plane came to rest in the Outer Port Anchorage making a low and splendid landing, at 10.25 am.

"In a few minutes the big plane had been tied to the landing raft, and the Macao Health Officer, Dr Mesquita, boarded the plane immediately after which, headed by Mr A.E. La Porte, the officers of the Clipper came ashore. They were greeted by Mr K.A. Kennedy, representing the community. . . . His Excellency Dr Tamagnini Barbosa said that in welcoming the first plane of the regular service of the Pan-American airways, he joined in the general rejoicing over the successful accomplishment of the first flight of one of the Company's planes, and he expressed the hope that every subsequent flight would be blessed with like success and good fortune.

"After chatting with the Governor for a few minutes, the officials of the Pan-American Company invited His Excellency to visit the plane and, accompanied by (several officials he) entered and inspected

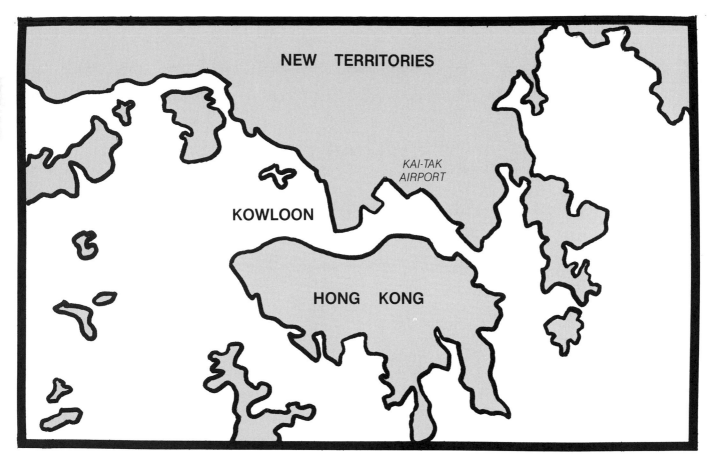

the plane.

"Immediately afterwards, His Excellency the Governor wished Mr La Porte and the officers a pleasant trip, after which Mr Kennedy went up to the Governor and thanked him again for all his interest, and the Clipper cast off at 11.23 am and by 11.26 am had taken off from the water on its way to Hongkong, and was soon lost to sight."

The *Post* also described the Clipper's arrival in Hong Kong:

"Over 4000 persons witnessed one of the momentous events in the history of commercial aviation and of Hongkong yesterday morning at Kai Tak—the landing of the Hongkong Clipper on Kowloon Bay on the conclusion of its flight from Manila, thus inaugurating round-the-world air service connection.

"The 23-ton plane came gracefully to a stop only a short distance from the shore and the dream of aviators, businessmen and travellers for many years had been realised."

For about a year, the Clippers used Macao as the terminus of the trans-Pacific flights, but they landed briefly at Hong Kong, a city that was regarded as an intermediate stop on the route. By early 1937, however, Pan Am had reached an agreement with the British for terminal landing rights at Hong Kong. In April of that year, Clippers began to fly directly from Manila to Hong Kong with the blessings of local officials. (Macao was non-schedule until 1937.)

The Clippers landed at Kai-tak Airport on the Kowloon side of Victoria Harbor. The airport had been established in 1934 as a land and seaplane base; in addition to CNAC and Imperial Airways, it served Air France and offered connecting flights from Hong Kong to Europe via Asia and India.

At the time, Hong Kong was a city of nearly one million, and was a gateway to China as well as a Far Eastern base of operations for Western businesses. While Hong Kong had been ceded by China to the British in 1864, it did not gain commercial importance until the opening of the Suez Canal in 1869. The canal's opening brought Hong Kong closer to Europe via ship; the Clipper route would bring the city—and Asia—closer to America via airplane.

In order to keep the M-130s on a two-week, round-trip schedule from California to Manila, Pan Am decided to use an S-42B for the final 546-mile leg from Manila to Hong Kong. Renamed the *Hong Kong Clipper*, the plane could easily make this relatively short distance, carrying 32 passengers. Sometimes an M-130 would fly all the way to Hong Kong; once put into service, the B-314s also made the trip.

The Clipper service to Hong Kong lasted until Dec. 8, 1941, when the *Hong Kong Clipper*, docked at Kai-tak, was destroyed by Japanese planes. Today, very little remains of the Clipper operations at Hong Kong and Macao. All traces of the Hong Kong operation have disappeared beneath a runway extension at Kai-tak Airport. In Macao, the Clipper terminal building is intact, now used as a yacht club.

The *Philippine Clipper* first arrived in Macao on Oct. 23, 1936. Here, as elsewhere, large crowds gathered to greet the plane. Macao was used as a temporary base while landing rights were attained in Hong Kong. The Pan Am terminal, still standing, is used as a yacht club today.   PAA

An older form of transportation sits off the pier at Macao.

The direction finder at Macao, and a partial view of the city.

6632-1595N-6)(11-29-35-3-50P)(10-900) CHINA CLIPPER
OF FIRST TRANS

PAA

...D TO P.A.A. LANDING STAGE, MANILA P.I., AFTER COMPLETION
...C FLIGHT, NOV. 29, 1935. (MANILA HOTEL IN BACKGROUND)

PACIFIC SURVEY FLIGHTS

The first leg of the proposed Clipper route, the section from San Francisco to Hawaii, had been left largely unexplored by aviators. A few pilots had flown it, but the route had never been attempted by a commercial airline and certainly not by a flying boat.

Thus when Pan Am first discussed the possibility of sending flying boats on survey flights over the route, the idea was met with some opposition from the airline's board of directors. Two directors resigned over Trippe's insistence on the survey flights and the possibility of a trans-Pacific route.

A Sikorsky S-42 (#NR-823M), named the *Pan American Clipper*, was to be used for the first survey flights. Before undertaking the Pacific flights, Capt. Musick and his crew, using Florida as a base, logged many hours over the Atlantic. On one flight, they took the Clipper on a 2,600-mile round-trip between Florida and the Virgin Islands to simulate the distance from California to Hawaii. The plane eventually was brought to the West Coast, where Musick and his crew—Sullivan, Wright, Canaday, Noonan and Jarboe—put in weeks flying up and down the California coast to familiarize themselves with the terrain.

On April 16, 1935, at 3:30 p.m., the *Pan American Clipper* lifted off the waters of San Francisco Bay and headed toward Hawaii. Usually, first flights are attended by much ceremony and publicity, but on this occasion there were no cheering crowds, blowing sirens, or bursting bombs. Only the ground personnel and the crewmen's wives were there to bid the plane good-bye.

The flight lasted 18 hours and nine minutes, with no problems encountered en route. Every hour, Musick radioed a report back to California, and news of the plane's progress was then sent out all over the world. As it approached Hawaii, the Clipper flew past Diamond Head, past downtown Honolulu, and touched down in Pearl Harbor, mooring at the Naval Air Station on Ford Island. It was greeted by large crowds and news reporters, and the plane's crew were welcomed with the traditional Hawaiian lei ceremony.

Musick and his crew had proved beyond a doubt that the Pacific route was feasible—at least as far as Hawaii. At this time, Clippers could not fly farther west—Midway, the second stop on the proposed route, was still receiving shipments of supplies to build a base, while Wake Island, the third stop, was still bare atoll.

Crew of S-42, NR-823M, the *Pan American Clipper,* at Alameda before taking off for the first survey flight to Hawaii on April 16, 1935. The map they are holding shows the route from California to Hawaii.
PAA

Four days after the Clipper's arrival in Honolulu, Musick headed the plane back toward California. In 1935, however, the science of over-water weather forecasting was still in its infancy, and the Clipper encountered headwinds that were stronger than anticipated. During the flight, it became obvious that the plane's ground speed was under 100 mph and concern grew that the Clipper might not have enough fuel to make the California coast. The plane, according to its schedule, was also overdue.

Finally, the crew sighted the coast, and the Clipper made a perfect landing on San Francisco Bay. When the engineer checked the fuel tanks, he found about 72 gallons of gas left. It had been a close call. The airline downplayed the danger, stating that the plane had intentionally made some detours along the coast to increase the time spent in the air. As weather forecasting improved, so the logic went, the headwinds could be anticipated and dealt with.

Three additional flights were made by the S-42 *Pan American Clipper.* The second flight left June 12 for Hawaii and Midway, and the third flight left Aug. 9 for Hawaii, Midway, and Wake. The last flight departed on Oct. 5 for Hawaii, Midway, Wake, and Guam, while the final leg of the route, Guam to Manila, was never flown by a survey plane.* The last two survey flights were captained by R.O.D. Sullivan; Musick was preparing the new Martin 130 for the historic first flight all the way from San Francisco to Manila.

Capt. Edwin Musick stands before the S-42 just before his historic first survey flight to Hawaii on April 16, 1935.   PAA

---

*See appendix for survey flight information.

This rare photo shows the *Pan American Clipper* taking off from Alameda on the afternoon of April 16, 1935, for the initial survey flight to Hawaii.
John Johnson, Groton, Conn.

The *Pan American Clipper* wings her way over San Francisco and the uncompleted San Francisco-Oakland Bay Bridge on the afternoon of April 16, 1935. Yerba Buena Island can be seen on the left.

PAA

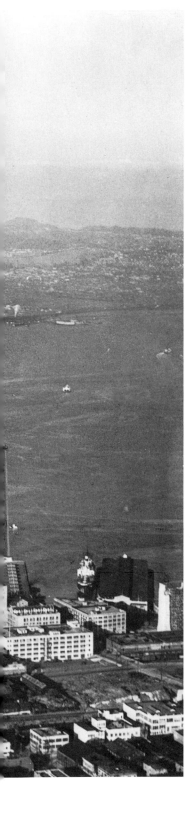

On her way to a landing at Pearl Harbor, the plane passes by a Hawaiian landmark, Diamond Head, and then-undeveloped Waikiki. On the left are signatures of the crew.   PAA

Landing at the Naval Air Station on Ford Island, the plane is greeted by a crowd of civilians, naval personnel and news media. Sailors in bathing suits helped attach the beaching gear to the plane.   Pearl Harbor Library

First Officer R.O.D. Sullivan hands the first sack of mail from the plane to Honolulu Postmaster John H. Wilson at Ford Island while naval personnel look on.   HA

Capt. Musick gets his share of leis and a letter of welcome.   HA

The crew of the S-42 receive a traditional Hawaiian welcome. Left to right: W.T. Jarboe, Jr., radioman; Harry E. Canaday, junior officer; R.O.D. Sullivan, first officer; Capt. Edwin Musick; Fred J. Noonan, navigator; Victor A. Wright, chief engineer.

Capt. Musick with the commander of the Pearl Harbor Naval Base. PAA

The crew poses with civilian and military dignitaries of Hawaii after a successful first survey flight. PAA

The S-42 passes by the Honolulu harbor on its way back to San Francisco.   NA

FIRST AIRMAIL FLIGHT

The afternoon of Nov. 22, 1935, was clear and bright at Alameda, Pan Am's Pacific base, just across the bay from San Francisco. Final checks were being conducted for a flight that would make history in more than one respect.

The new Martin M-130, the *China Clipper*, had never flown the Pacific. And even though her predecessor, the S-42, had made several flights, the flight that would begin the afternoon of November 22 would be the first to travel as far as Manila. This first flight would only carry mail between San Francisco and Manila, but it would pave the way for future flights that would carry not only mail, but passengers.

That the *China Clipper* had already captured the imagination of the American public could easily be seen that afternoon. Hundreds of cars were parked on an adjacent landing field, and a crowd of more than 25,000 people lined the shore. Thousands more watched from San Francisco to see the first *Clipper* fly across the bay.

There were a wealth of dignitaries on hand to send off the *Clipper,* including Juan Trippe, founder and president of Pan American Airways, and Postmaster General James Farley. The afternoon ceremonies that preceded the takeoff were broadcast around the world by radio. Stations at every stop along the way, from Honolulu to Manila, gave the word that they awaited the plane's arrival.

Even the president of the United States, Franklin Delano Roosevelt, could be counted as a fan of the *China Clipper*, sending a message that read in part: "[This is] a century of progress that is without parallel, and it is our just pride that America and Americans have played no minor part in the blazing of new trails."

Bags of letters had been flown from across the country by United Air Lines and Transcontinental and Western Air Lines. Now, to mark the progress of which President Roosevelt spoke, the letters were transferred to an old stagecoach, the likes of which had been employed to carry the mail less than 50 years before. From the stagecoach, the letters were transferred on board the *China Clipper*, 110,000 of them totaling 1,879 pounds.

"Captain Musick, you have your sailing orders. Cast off and depart for Manila in accordance therewith."

The *China Clipper* was flown west to Alameda in early November of 1935. Here, she is docked at the San Diego Naval Air Station on Nov. 11 before leaving for her final hop to Alameda.   NA

With these words spoken by Juan Trippe, the *China Clipper* taxied onto San Francisco Bay. A crew of nine had been scheduled to make this inaugural flight. Five crew members were veterans of the survey flights: Capt. Edwin Musick; First Officer R.O.D. Sullivan; Engineering Officer V.A. Wright; Navigator Fred Noonan, and First Radio Officer W.T. Jarboe. Second Officer George King and Second Engineering Officer C.D. Wright were aboard for training purposes. Due to last minute changes, Second Radio Officer T.R. Runnells and Second Junior Flight Officer Max Werber were left behind, reducing the crew to seven.

The first leg of the journey would be the longest, some 2400 miles from San Francisco west to Honolulu. But Honolulu must have been the farthest thing from Captain Musick's mind when, upon takeoff, he found himself unable to gain enough altitude to clear the San Francisco-Oakland Bay Bridge. On her first flight, the *China Clipper* passed beneath the cables of the as-yet-uncompleted bridge, followed closely by the aircraft of her military escort. Only later did the public learn that this was not meant to be a regular part of the *Clipper's* route.

Unlike the Bay Bridge, the weather proved to be cooperative, with nothing more serious than scattered clouds near the Hawaiian coast. The *Clipper* was able to keep radio contact with Pan Am's stations in California, Hawaii and Midway. With safety uppermost in the minds of the crew, additional radio contacts were made with a number of ships at sea, including a Coast Guard cutter, a U.S. warship and a freight steamer.

On November 23, after a 17-hour flight, the *Clip-per* landed at Pearl Harbor at 10:19 a.m. The first leg had been completed without a hitch, a fact that was not lost on the crowd that had gathered to greet the *Clipper* and her crew. The mail destined for Hawaii was unloaded, and more mail destined for the Philippines was loaded in its place. Crates of fresh food were also stowed on board to be delivered to the Pan Am facilities on Midway and Wake for Thanksgiving dinner.

On Sunday morning, November 23, at 6:35 a.m., the *Clipper* began the second leg of her maiden voyage. Fourteen passengers—Pan Am employees on their way to Midway and Wake to relieve the crews there—took off for Midway to the cheers of hundreds of people aboard small boats in the harbor and gathered along the shore. The second leg was to prove as uneventful as the first. The plane cruised beneath a cloud layer at 2000 feet until, 13 hours and 30 minutes later, at 2:00 p.m., she broke into clear skies and landed just one minute off schedule.

The next morning, nine additional non-revenue passengers came on board, and at 6:12 a.m., Monday, November 25, Capt. Musick began the third leg of his flight. The flight to Wake took 12 hours and 26 minutes, during which the crew maintained radio contact with the Wake station and with a Matson liner, the *S.S. President Lincoln*. However, as the *Clipper* crossed the international dateline on this leg of her journey, she arrived at Wake on Tuesday, November 26, at 1:38 p.m. Most of this flight was governed by instruments due to a dense cloud cover.

On Wednesday, November 27, the *Clipper* left Wake for Guam. The plane's altitude ranged from

With hundreds of cars parked on the flying field and spectators gathered at the water's edge (on the right), the *China Clipper* is about to take off on her historic flight to Manila. This flight marked the beginning of commercial air service across the Pacific.

PAA

To symbolize the historic event, bags of mail are brought to the plane by stagecoach, thus representing the past and the future of mail service.   PAA

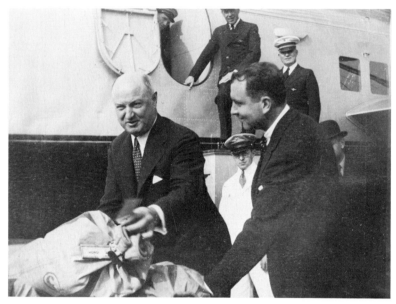

Middle: U.S. Postmaster General James A. Farley (left) and Juan Trippe, president of Pan American Airways System, inspect the mail bags that make up the cargo of the inaugural transoceanic flight to Manila. Bottom: Farley helps stack the mail bags before the official ceremonies.   PAA

Mail ready for loading aboard the Clipper. Capt. Musick stands on the steps while Farley and Trippe look on.   PAA

Postmaster General Farley announces the start of regular airmail service across the Pacific.   PAA

Newspapers around the world carry headlines of the first airmail flight from California to Manila.   PAA

MANILA — GUAM 1450 MI. — WAKE 1242 MI. MIDWAY — 1380 MI. HAWAII — 2410 MILES — SAN FRANCISCO
1500 MI.

COMPARATIVE TEMPERATURES

San Francisco Chronicle
THE CITY'S ONLY HOME-OWNED NEWSPAPER

WEATHER
Fair, With Clouds

FOUNDED 1865—VOL. CXLVII. NO. 151   CCC   SAN FRANCISCO, CAL., SATURDAY, NOVEMBER 23, 1935   DAILY 5 CENTS, SUNDAY 10 CENTS

Clues Show Manno Firm Sold Barrel Of Fluoride

Deadly Powder Believed Shipped Through Error

Mystery Expected to Be Cleared Up Soon

Clues indicating that the poison which killed three persons and imperiled several hundred when sold as soda in a Mission street store, came directly from the basement of the Manno Sales Company, assertedly were in the hands of police last night.

Inspector George Engler of the homicide squad made this statement after day long investigation:

"I am convinced that one barrel containing deadly fluoride was mistakenly included in the shipment of six barrels of supposed baking soda, sold by the Manno firm to Rosenthal's.

"From various bits of evidence gathered, I am further convinced that fluoride barrel was the one used to refill the barrels of uncontaminated soda as they were depleted through sales to customers of the Rosenthal store.

"I intend to act at once on my conviction and expect to have a definite announcement to make that will clear up the mystery."

Engler's theory was fortified by interrogation of an employe of Nick Manno, proprietor of the salvage firm and of Rosenthal.

EMPLOYE QUIZZED

From August J. Weber, employed at Manno's, the inspector obtained this statement:

"I painted three barrels of soda on our truck first, they were delivered to Rosenthal's. Then the driver made a second trip. This time three more barrels were brought up from the basement. I don't know what was in them. Nanno stuck his finger in one, tasted the stuff and said that's soda, take it along."

Proceeding to Rosenthal's, Engler questioned Jack Dineen, and reported the latter made this declaration:

"I am certain that the barrel we got back from the cooper to whom we sold it was one of the barrels that came from Manno's."

FLUORIDE IN BARREL

The barrel referred to had the residue of a white substance still in it when it was returned, an the cooper tested which said the contents were death-dealing fluoride, proved to be death-dealing fluoride.

Dineen said Dineen further explained:

"Then the contents of that barrel
(Continued on Page 3, Col. 3)

Doris Cromwell Marks Birthday

HONOLULU, Hawaii, Nov. 22 (P) — Doris Duke Cromwell, generally considered the world's richest girl, quietly observed her 23d birthday today, happily married and eager to keep out of the limelight.

♦ Small Apartments
Turn to the
★ Chronicle Want Ad Pages

——AND HISTORY IS MADE!

China Clipper shown as she soared out of S. F. Bay and over the Golden Gate bridge on her maiden flight to Hawaii and the Philippines.

Officer Aboard Clipper Describes Pacific Hop

Engines Drone Steadily, Men Go About Duties Like Clockwork

By GEORGE KING
Second Flight Officer of the China Clipper, Writing for United Press

ABOARD THE CHINA CLIPPER, EN ROUTE TO HONOLULU, Nov. 22—As the sun goes down, casting a flaming mantle over bulbous clouds beneath, scattered strips of cumulus high above the circular world sink into impenetrable blackness.

A cloudy ceiling shuts off the stars, and the clouds below shut off the Pacific swells 7000 feet below.

They pilot lights seen through the flight deck grow brighter. The radium painted dials on the 187 flight and engine instruments on the board glow eerily.

A faint yellow point of light on Radio Officer Jarvis's receiver blinks with his Morse fire transmission of the position brief of major position reports back to the base at San Francisco ahead to Honolulu to Midway to Wake to Guam and to Manila thereafter.

Child Poisoned By Burglar Loot

PATERSON, N. J., Nov. 22 — A quirk of fate today killed a child of three by the aftermath of a burglary.

Robert Maver died after eating poison tablets. They were thrown in his backyard when the thieves discarded them during a midnight rendezvous.

Wed Day, Sailor Leaps to His Death

SANTA BARBARA, Nov. 22 (P) — Henry Morse, Livermore man, who was to have been married today to Mrs. Marie Warren, leaped to his death from the Santa Barbara Hotel here.

Giant China Clipper Hops For Manila

25,000 Watch Huge Airship Take Off From Bay on Epochal Flight

Inaugurates Plane Service From S. F. to Orient

By ROYCE BRIER

America's history and the world's reached some giant new age yesterday when the China Clipper took flight with the trans-Pacific mail and a prophet of old would be needed to foretell it.

The Clipper soared from Alameda Airport at 3:47 p.m., lifting slowly and spreading proudly her silver wings against the setting sun, flashing 150 years of Yankee tradition in her propeller blades.

Five minutes later she passed through the Golden Gate and at 11 o'clock she was 820 miles down the Western sea.

25,000 WATCH

Twenty-five thousand people—such an outpouring as the Bay District has never given an airplane—waved her good-bye. There were 7000 at the airport, where a brief ceremony preceded the departure, and other thousands were at the Marine and on the San Francisco's housetops.

Their acclaim was given to an idea rather than to aviation audacity, for Captain Musick and his crew of six are piloting the most advanced airliner of the day, over a course charted and proof as mass as mass technical ingenuity can make it against the unforeseen.

It is the unfathomable future latent in this week and coming machine, not the 25,000 that American Airways plant that there are the sea which links the drama and the saga.

BON VOYAGE FETE

Something of this was manifest in the huge voyage ceremony, and it was stamped with clarity on the faces of the thousand who watched. Outside the air harbor when she was a mere wink the Clipper droned out its an outside explosive. She taped a mile off. an hour warming up her four motors until one clean fist seemed very far below. The Clipper was gone.

The crew's send for thousands cheered at the Clipper point at the moment of her rise. Thirty planes had been for line overhead and they dropped toward the monarch beneath.
(Continued on Page 3 Col. 3)

Betting Odds Favor Bears In Big Game

Greatest Grid Throng in Coast History Revels on Eve of Palo Alto Battle

90,000 to See Struggle at 'Farm'; Tickets Gobbled Up

History's biggest sports crowd on the Pacific Coast surged into San Francisco and neighboring cities last night jubilantly celebrating the eve of the 43d annual coronation ceremony of King Football.

The king's 1935 reign ends at Palo Alto this afternoon.

While 90,000 cheering loyal subjects acclaim his greatest predepression season from the seats of Stanford stadium, the football teams of University of California and Stanford will enact their annual pageant in the king's honor.

Last minute odds quoted by bookmakers indicated the California continues to rule as favorite.

18 SPECIAL TRAINS

BECAUSE OF THE super-stupendously-released crowds expected at the Big Game, special transportation has been arranged.

The Southern Pacific announces 18 special trains of 12 coaches each, starting at 10 o'clock this morning from Third and Townsend streets. They will load and get away when full. The last run will arrive about 1:30 o'clock. This service will be additional to the six regular trains.

Similarly six extra trains will leave Oakland starting at the same hour. The last one leaving at 11:50 and arriving at 1:30 p.m.

Similar return service will be given after the game, the company announces.

5 TO 4 ON BEARS

Five to four odds the undefeated united Golden Bears will be the unanimous choice for Rose Bowl honors.

Bookmakers by steamer by train by automobile and went out some more than 100,000 party and rooters. Most of them had arrived a night but additional thousands were coming highway straining transports upon bus lines and adding to railroad Special was the apparent far out of fresno at 6 o'clock this afternoon.

Scalpers prices skyrocketed as it became known as the game good seats had been sold. These will be snapped up at stadium booths University authorities were quietly checking tickets good seats were being retailed for as high as $100 a pair.

GAYETY RULES

Hotels and houses were jammed Most city reservations were exhausted. Florists worked late into the night filling rush orders Cocktail bars were packed to the doors.

Added pep was given celebrations of down town crowds when the California band, resplendent in full uniform, cavorted through the business district streets and lobbies while the crowds roared the choruses of favorite college airs. Queen Gayety was being acclaimed consort of King Football.

PLAYING FIELD FAST

Stanford's playing field was reported to be fast and dry and was expected to remain in ideal condition with the announcement its weather forecasters that the day would be fair and mild.

Can California check Stanford's plunging All-American Bobby Grayson or Wanford's All-American Monk Moscrip whose game last year has three times the Cards this year by goals from twist?

Can the great California passer Floyd Blower be checked in his attempted goal line dash slants?

Mad gaf, delirious fans?

Expectant, nervous, too the mouth day.

Historical afternoon?

The Big Game of 1935!

U.S. Puts Pressure On Ship Lines to Halt War Trading

Threat of Financial Reprisal Made by Shipping Board

Exports to Italians Gain Despite Embargo

WASHINGTON, Nov. 22 (P)—The financial pressure of a principal mortgage holder was applied, in effect, to the shipping industry today by the Administration to prevent shipments of potential war materials to Italy and Ethiopia.

An implied threat by the Shipping Board to become a tough creditor was reported to have held in port several vessels already loaded with supplies for the East African war zone.

EXPORTS SHOW RISE

Even as this move was disclosed a sharp jump in exports to Italy during October was shown in newly compiled Commerce Department figures. Despite the frequent admonition of neutrality pleas in both President Roosevelt and Secretary Hull intended to prevent shipments of any character to the belligerent there were exports to Italy were:

October, $6,821,366; September, $4,735,887.

It was on October 5 that the President proclaimed American ships which carried implements of arms and ammunition, and the export of the free might be covered by the warning condition. Some shippers saw the apparent failure of this move to prevent exporting leading to the more hard way.

THREAT IN LETTERS

The hinted threat to steamship owners and operators was inclosed in letters from the Shipping Board Bureau to lines owing money to the Government. In itself, the letter was given over principally as a reiteration that the Administration's neutrality policy deeply opposes all commerce with the belligerents.

On another front, Jesse W. Donaldson, Postoffice deputy in charge of ocean mail, said no action has been proposed to stop possible violations of the embargo by ocean mail contract carriers.

300 Latins Slain
Africa Cite Victory
In 11-Hour Battle

ADDIS ABABA, Nov. 22 (P) — An official communique said the 11 hour battle reputedly fought in the Wamberta Tembien region north of Makale was the first real fighting on any scale since the war began.

The government also announced a battle in the Tembien mountain region in which an Italian commander and many of his men were said to have been killed when they were surprised by Ethiopian forces while advancing on Makale.
Additional War News on Page 16

For a "Big Game" Thrill
DRIVE THE New BUICK

Touch the throttle of the new Buick and things happen. The take-off is instant fast. No laboring pause, no shiver, just that silk smooth swing into speed.

You head into the open straightaway. Soon you are traveling faster by plenty than you realize.

It's as thrilling as a 40 yard run to a touchdown. But never the thrill of hazard. The thrill, rather of beautifully poised mechanism doing what ever you want done without effort or strain.

See this new Buick today — drive it, and sample that thrill for yourself.

HOWARD AUTOMOBILE CO.
VAN NESS AT CALIFORNIA
SAN FRANCISCO

California's new unemployment insurance law, affecting hundreds of thousands of employers and employes becomes operative January 1, 1936. The State law is complementary to the new Federal social security act. The provisions of the new law will be outlined in a series of articles by Earl Behrens in The Chronicle, beginning Sunday.

Czech President Plans to Resign

PRAGUE, Czechoslovakia, Nov. 22 (P)—President Thomas Masaryk of the Czechoslovakian republic plans to resign immediately.

1200 to 2000 feet, as she once again encountered pleasant weather. In 14 hours the *Clipper* reached Guam, landing off of Orote Point near Sumay at 3:05 p.m.

In order to keep to her original schedule, which called for the *China Clipper* to end her journey by landing on Manila Bay on November 29, the plane and her crew remained in Guam on Thursday, November 28. On Friday, at 6:12 a.m., the *Clipper* took off from a rough sea without incident. After a flight of 14 hours and 20 minutes under ceilings ranging from 6000 to 8000 feet, she appeared over her final destination, Manila, where her historic journey would be completed. As the *Clipper* flew over the city, the residents of Manila came out of their homes to watch. A crowd of several hundred thousand lined up on the waterfront at Luneta Park across from the Manila Hotel to greet the plane. The *Clipper* circled the hotel before landing on Manila Bay.

There, she tied up to a float that had been brought up from Cavite, and was surrounded by dozens of small boats that, in their skippers' excitement, circled dangerously close to the *Clipper*'s wings. U.S. military planes flew overhead, adding their own welcome to that of the people of Manila.

Nov. 29, 1935, would be a memorable day in Philippine history, as it marked the islands' first air link with the United States. A floral arch awaited the crew at Luneta Park, and buildings throughout Manila were decorated for the occasion. The city treated the crew of the *Clipper* to a triumphant ticker-tape parade.

Musick's words upon the arrival of the *China Clipper* in Manila, displayed the optimism that technological progress would improve relations between East and West.

First mail flight at Pearl Harbor, Nov. 23, 1935.

HA

"We deeply appreciate the enthusiastic welcome you have given us. I do not need to tell you that we are very happy to be in Manila—to have completed on a schedule actually set nearly five years ago—the first trans-Pacific crossing—a flight which, at that time, was considered by many to be impossible.

We in the *China Clipper,* have come across eight thousand six hundred miles of ocean to the Philippines. Sent off from San Francisco with colorful ceremonies, by which the people of America wished to express, through us, a personal greeting to their neighbors, the people of the East, we have received royal tributes at each of our brief stopping points en route, each symbolizing that same expression of friendship, good-will and the hope of peaceful, prosperous, happy relations between the peoples of two continents which, from today on, are to be neighbors in fact as well as in spirit.

Although your honors are expressed to us, we are keenly aware that we were privileged to be aboard the *China Clipper*, we are but the representatives of the American people whose strong urge for better and closer cultural and commercial relations with the peoples of the Philippines and the East, brought this service into being. And particularly, are we aware of that splendid functioning organization of Pan American Airways whose untiring efforts, whose ceaseless watch and alert aid alone made such an important undertaking possible.

Today's flight is not the result of a simple process. Five years of ceaseless planning, designing and construction, training and practice have advanced aviation to this point where today it is possible for us to span an ocean, where heretofore air transport service has only crossed narrow channels. The rich reward of sweeping away that age-old barrier of distance between the new world and the old, between the East and the West, has been the inspiration through which this great achievement has been made.

It is the sincere hope of the Pan American Airways System that this air service, inaugurated today, may bring rich benefits to the Commonwealth of the Philippines, to the countries of the Orient, in the peace, prosperity and continued progress that is the hope of the American people.

Mr. President, we are particularly honored to present to you the first trans-Pacific air mail letter in the history of the world—a personal message from our president, the Honorable Franklin D. Roosevelt, to you sir. This letter has come to you—nearly 12,000 miles—in scarcely seven days after leaving the White House.

Thank you, Mr. President. It is particularly fitting that the establishment of the first trans-Pacific air mail service, marking a new era in the relations between the East and the West should so closely follow the institution of the Commonwealth of the Islands of the Philippines. It must, sir, in no small measure, form a tribute to you whose vision and unflagging efforts have done so much to bring it into being. Thank you."

The plane circles over Manila Bay before making her descent into the waters of the bay near the Manila Hotel's inlet. She landed at 3:30 p.m., six days after leaving Alameda (59 hours, 48 minutes flying time).
PAA

Thousands of spectators line the seawall around Luneta Park in Manila awaiting the arrival of the *China Clipper* on Nov. 29, 1935.

The *China Clipper*'s history-making flight from California to Manila had taken 59 hours and 48 minutes, remarkably close to the 60 hours that Pan Am had estimated for the 8,210-mile trip. A three-week journey by boat could now be completed in less than a third of the time, opening the door to new opportunities for businessmen and tourists alike.

Capt. Musick was able to underscore the significance of this flight in a dramatic way, presenting the president of the Commonwealth of the Philippines, Manuel Quezon, with a letter from President Roose-

velt that had left San Francisco less than six days before. President Quezon responded with a letter that would be carried back to President Roosevelt on the *Clipper*'s return flight.

The *Clipper* spent two days in Manila preparing for her return trip. As fuel and mail were taken on board, the crew was at times overwhelmed by the acts of generosity shown them by the Filipino people. Then, on Monday, December 2, at 2:53 a.m., the *China Clipper* began her flight back to San Francisco. The return trip proceeded without incident, the crew and her

As she splashes down in the bay, dozens of small craft join the plane for her final taxi to the floating dock. PAA

cargo encountering nothing worse than a bit of bad weather on the Guam to Wake leg. At Midway, 18 Pan Am personnel came on board for Honolulu.

In order to arrive back in Alameda during daylight hours on the sixth, the plane had to leave Honolulu at 3:02 a.m. on Thursday, December 5. A cloud cover over San Francisco once again forced the plane to navigate by instruments, but her crew brought her in safely at 10:36 a.m., Friday, December 6. In fact, the *Clipper* landed considerably ahead of schedule due to favorable trade winds.

The return trip had taken 63 hours and 24 minutes, while the entire 16,420-mile trip had taken 123 hours, 12 minutes of flying time. In just two weeks, Captain Musick and his crew had made the world a much smaller place.

Military planes fly in formation over the clipper while spectators stand on top of the Manila Hotel for a better view.　PAA

The welcoming banquet was held at the Manila Hotel with the table arranged in the outline of the flying boat.
　PAA

Today's view from The Manila Hotel is the same as the 1935 view. Additional buildings have been erected on the dock area to the right.

The plane ties up at the floating dock in Manila Bay after her historic flight. PAA

As did the residents of Honolulu, the people of Manila create a festive atmosphere for the crew. A welcome arch is set up in Luneta Park, to be followed by a parade through Manila. PAA

The clipper ties up to the floating dock in Manila Bay, Nov. 29, 1935.　　　　　　　NA

An unusual rear view of the *China Clipper* tied to the floating dock in Manila Bay.　　　　PAA

"CLIPPER" ARRIVAL in ROTOGRAVURE PICTORIAL—in this ISSUE

18 PAGES

The Tribune

ALL THE NEWS — ALL THE TIME

The WEATHER

YEAR XI. NO. 207 — MANILA, PHILIPPINES, SATURDAY, NOVEMBER 30, 1935

'CLIPPER' COMPLETES EPOCHAL HOP

Italy to Attack British Fleet If Oil Ban Is Applied

Mussolini Says 'Death Squads' Will Annihilate English Mediterranean Armada

LAVAL GIVES WARNING

France to Support Britain If Duce Makes Desperate Move

By Associated Press

Paris, Nov. 29. — Responsible sources of [illegible] said tonight that a world war was impending if League of Nations members placed an oil embargo on Italy.

Ready to Quit League

Premier Benito Mussolini was said to have outlined a swift thrust at the British fleet in the Mediterranean if the League placed sanctions on oil to Italy. It was said that Mussolini would withdraw his diplomats from "enemy" countries, resign from the League and attack the British fleet with "death squads." It was said that the Fascist grand council adopted this program during a midnight session Nov. 28.—The Italian cabinet is due to meet at 10 a.m., Nov. 29.

125 "Death" Pilots

It was said that Premier Pierre Laval, of France, has destroyed Mussolini's hopes for further postponement of the oil embargo when he yielded to insistent demands that he inform the Italian ambassador that if Mussolini did anything "desperate" in the Mediterranean France and other league members would unreservedly sup-

(Continued on page 7)

Nation Honors Great Plebeian

ANDRES BONIFACIO

The Great Plebeian whose birthday will be celebrated by the entire nation today

(Details on page 7)

BOARD KILLS ZONE MEASURE

Study of Eight Years Wasted—Crisis Faces Council—Fuente Disappointed

The proposed zonification ordinance which was prepared after an 8-year study and investigation by many elements in Manila, was killed by the municipal board yesterday afternoon.

The disapproval of the measure provoked a crisis in the city council and the break up of the present majority composed of eight councilors. It was said that a new majority may be formed.

In local political circles the disapproval of the measure was looked upon with suspicion.

Disappointed at the result of the voting, President Manuel de la Fuente who had set his heart on the enactment of a zoning measure, condemned the attitude of some of the councilors as he spoke from the rostrum. He later told news-

(Continued on page 1)

QUEZON AIMS TO RUB OUT BANDITS

Constabulary Told to Make Islands Safe from Outlaw Menace

Determined to stamp out banditry and communism in Laguna and Tayabas, considered the hotbed of communistic organizations, President Quezon yesterday evening told newspapermen that he had given instructions that constabulary forces should remain stationed near the mountains of those provinces, where towns and barrios are menaced by bandits until the threat has been entirely wiped out.

The President contemplates establishing permanent constabulary stations in various places in Tayabas until such time as the situation is fully under control. He said that the soldiers will have to remain there until banditry is fully wiped out.

"The bandits and those communists there have to stop their foolishness," the President empha-

(Continued on page 3)

NIPPON ARMY BLAMED FOR SPLIT OF CHINA

Sharp Protests, Charges Filed At Embassy—All Blame Denied

By Associated Press

Tokyo, Nov. 29.—It was officially learned today that efforts of Occidental diplomats, including supporters of the Nine Power Treaty, had learned of Japan's intentions toward North China and how plans to fulfill treaty obligations had met the barriers of Oriental evasiveness combined with an attitude of injured innocence.

All inquiries met denial that the Japanese were responsible for the separatist movement in North China. The Japanese said that the nine power treaty was not involved.

By Associated Press

Nanking, Nov. 2.—In a sharply worded protest, the Chinese gov-

(Continued on page 4)

GILHOUSER'S DAUGHTER IS KILLED IN CRASH

By Associated Press

Stockton, Calif., Nov. 24.—Margaret Gilhouser, 20, daughter of Mr. and Mrs. Gilhouser, who are en route to Manila, was killed and three of her University of California classmates were injured in an automobile collision here today.

Among the injured was Jean McCorriston, 18, of Honolulu. She was hurt internally.

Heavy Voting Is Feature

Millions of Ballots Held In Reserve for Closing Days of Contest

As there are only 15 days left from today for the election of the 25 finalists in the 1936 Woman's Popularity Contest sponsored by the TVT Newspapers, leaders of some of the candidates begin casting a great number of votes in the daily counting.

However, it is difficult for any prophet to predict the probable 25 winners in view of the several million votes being withheld until the last hour. Another reason why it cannot be determined in advance the names of the candidates who will qualify on midnight of December 15 is the fact that no definite number of votes is required of

(Continued on page 7)

Dr. ELVIRA M. ROBLES

CEBU CEMENT OFFICIAL IS FOUND DEAD

H. M. Power, Portland Cement Firm Superintendent Dies From Gunshot Wound

Special to the TRIBUNE

Cebu, Nov. 29.—With a gun shot through the heart, believed to be self inflicted, the body of H. M. Power, superintendent of the Cebu Portland Cement company at Naga, Cebu, was found shortly after noon today in his house. A .32 caliber revolver owned by the deceased, was found lying near the body.

Suicide Case?

Although suicide was clearly apparent, the authorities had instituted a probe for other suppositions as there were no evident causes for the man to take his own life.

The provincial police also investigated reports that the deceased had been investing in stocks heavily of late and had suffered reverses.

The superintendent was missing at his office unusually this morning and a search was instituted. When they came upon the body, it had been dead for some time, examination revealed.

Power Popular

The deceased, survived by his wife who is on her way back from a trip to America, was popular in Cebu business circles and was member of the Cebu Rotary Club, Cebu Chamber of Commerce and the American Country Club.

Mr. Power was largely responsible for modernization and improvement of the cement factory and given close cooperation to the board of directors under Filipino management.

EXPENSE PROBE IS AGREED UPON

National Assembly to Eliminate Steering Committee—Rules Ready Monday

A committee of 17 members to form the commission of investigators of government expenditures, will be one of the new creations in the National Assemvly. The members of the committee now drafting the proposed rules of the National Assembly, have agreed on the creation of this body.

Another important change proposed in the new rules to govern the assembly, is the abolition of the steering or control committee which guided the work of past house of representatives. The powers of this committee will be mostly placed upon the committee on rules which will be presided over by the floor leader.

The committee of five which is drafting the rules of the assembly, composed of Floor Leader Francisco Enage, Assemblymen Gregorio Perfecto, Felipe Buencamino, Pedro Sabido, and Jose Zulueta, has been working hard every day since last Wednesday in order to put the proposed rules of the assembly in final shape for presentation before that body next Monday. The committee holds meetings every morning at the Legislative building, and devote the afternoons to individual study of propositions for inclusion in the proposed rules.

(Continued on page 3)

CLIPPER LETTER

California Businessman Hails Flight in Note to TVT

(Pictures on Page 6)

One of the several thousand letters which the China Clipper brought to Manila was addressed to the Sunday Tribune. The letter was written by John W. Parker, vice-president of the Durkee Famous Foods, Inc., a food manufacturing firm at Berkeley, California.

Writing to the TVT, Mr. Parker says:

"I have great pleasure in sending greetings to you on the first flight of the China Clipper.

"It is to be hoped that the establishing of this service so soon after the inauguration of the Philippine Commonwealth will mark closer relation if possible between the two countries.

"My interest in the Philippines has been great, and beyond a mere business nature. It will be a pleasure to continue serving your people whatever possible.

100,000 SEE GIANT PLANE LAND IN BAY; COMMANDER DECLARES ROUTE IS SAFE

Reveals Plans

Capt. Musick Tells Press Present Flight "Exploratory" In Nature

GATHERING DATA HERE

Trans-Pacific Safe With Modern Equipment, Clipper Commander Declares

"With present-day equipment, including ships as modern as the China and Philippine clippers, the danger of crossing the Pacific Ocean is completely eliminated."

Reporters Received

Thus spoke Captain Edwin C. Musick, commander of the China Clipper, in an interview he granted the press at his suite at the Manila Hotel last evening shortly after coming from Malacañang where he and his fellow aviators had gone to pay their respects to President Manuel L. Quezon.

7 Men in Crew

The ship arrived with a crew of seven men, including Captain Musick, and three employes of the Pan American Airways who will remain in Manila as members of the ground crew. All of them are staying at the Manila Hotel.

The China Clipper's crew, besides Captain Musick, are R. O. D. Sullivan, first officer; George King, second officer; C. D. Wright, first engineer; V. A. Wright, second engineer; Cedric Nooman, navigation officer; and W. T. Jarboe, Jr., radio officer.

Fine Weather Throughout

Captain Musick said that he had no complaint to make regarding the trip, the weather throughout the crossing, from Alameda to Manila having been favorable. There were a few squalls, he said, but these did not bother the plane the least.

He stated that he was in constant touch with Manila ever since the Clipper left Guam early yesterday morning. From reports furnished by the weather bureau, the local ground crew of the Clipper furnished Captain Musick with hourly weather conditions throughout the hop from Guam. According to him, the four legs of the hop were uneventful and each was as good as the other.

Takes Straight Course

"We left Guam at 6 o'clock this morning, it was already daylight," Captain Musick said. "We flew on a straight course to Manila. The island of Catanduanes, in Albay, was the first land we sighted in the Philippines.

"We struck Manila at an altitude of 10,000 feet, above the clouds. We circled once and came down to 7,000 feet before we saw our air escorts and the city. Mr. Sullivan and I were at the controls when we arrived."

According to Captain Musick, two pilots are always at the controls. After three hours, they are relieved by two other pilots.

"The present flight of the China Clipper to Manila," he said, "is in the nature of an exploratory expedition." He said that he gathered all necessary data for future use. Until all data are at hand, he said passenger service will not begin. "This is the policy of the company," he pointed out.

"We are not after speed records during these flights. The China Clipper is capable of making a speed of 180 miles an hour, but we never made that much. We averaged 140 miles during the flight from Alameda."

The China Clipper is scheduled to leave Manila for the return trip

(Continued on page 6)

NEXT MAIL DISPATCHES

TO UNITED STATES

Dec. 4, 1:30 p. m. "President Jackson"

Dec. 9, 2:30 p. m. "Empress of Russia"

Dec. 13, 2:30 p. m. "Silverray"

Dec. 14, 1:30 p. m. "President Wilson"

TO EUROPE VIA SIBERIA

Dec. 4, 1:30 p. m. "President Jackson"

TO EUROPE VIA SUEZ

Dec. 7, [illegible]

Surrounded by all sorts of water craft, whose occupants were curious to get a full view of the huge plane, the "China Clipper" is pictured here just after it had been moored to the barge in the Manila Bay upon its arrival from Guam yesterday afternoon. The nose of the "Clipper" can be seen touching the runaway (extreme left foreground) extending from the barge. Pier 7 is the background.

From One President to Another

(The following is the letter brought yesterday by the "China Clipper" for President Quezon from President Roosevelt.)

The White House, Washington

November 18, 1935

My dear Mr. President:

It is a great pleasure for me to send you this word of greeting by the first airplane to carry the mails between the Unitd States and the Philippine Islands.

I feel that the more rapid communications which will inevitably follow the inauguration of this service will result in increased benefits to the trade and intercourse between the United States and the Philippines.

I am my dear Mr. President,
Very sincerely yours,

(Sgd.) FRANKLIN D. ROOSEVELT

The Honorable Manuel L. Quezon
President of the Commonwealth of the Philippines
Manila

What Quezon Told Capt. Musick

Speech of President Quezon on the Occasion of the Arrival of the "China Clipper" November 29, 1935.

I am highly honored to receive this letter from the President. I want to take advantage of this opportunity to welcome you, Captain Musick and the other gentlemen who have made this wonderful flight. You have swept away forever the distance which from the beginning of time has separated the great continent of America from the beautiful islands of the Pacific. I hope that these new facilities for commerce, for travel, for international communication will contribute greatly to the progress and peace of this part of the world. I want to congratulate you, Captain Musick and you gentlemen for your wonderful flight and I hope that you will enjoy your stay in this proverbially hospitable city.

"Rich Benefits to Commonwealth"

(Speech delievered by Commander Edwin C. Musick, of the China Clipper, at the Admiral Landing yesterday afternoon in response to the speech of welcome given by Secretary Antonio de las Alas of public works and communications).

We deeply appreciate the enthusiastic welcome you have given us. I do not need to tell you that we are very happy to be in Manila—to have completed on a schedule actually set nearly five years ago—the first trans-Pacific crossing—a flight which, at that time, was considered by many to be impossible.

We, in the China Clipper, have come across eight thousand six hundred miles of ocean to the Philippines. Sent off from San Francisco with colorful ceremonies by which the people of America wished to express, through us, a personal greeting to their neighbors, the people of the east, we have received royal tributes at each of our brief stopping points en route, each symbolizing that same expression of friendship, good will and the hope of peaceful, prosperous, happy relations between the peoples of two continents which, from today on, are to be neighbors in fact as well as in spirit.

Although your honors are expressed to us, we are keenly aware that we are privileged to be aboard the China Clipper and are but the representatives of the American people whose strong urge for better and closer cultural and commercial relations with the peoples of the Philippines and the East, brought this service into being. And particularly, are we aware of that splendid functioning organization of Pan American Airways whose untiring efforts, whose ceaseless watch and alert aid alone made such important undertaking possible.

Today's flight is not the result of a simple process. Five years of ceaseless planning, designing and construction, training and practice have advanced aviation to this point where today it is possible for us to span an ocean, where heretofore air transport service has only crossed narrow channels. The rich reward of sweeping away that age-old barrier of distance between the new world and the old, between the East and the West, has been the inspiration through which this great achievement has been made.

It is the sincere hope of the Pan American Airways System that this air service inaugurated today, may bring rich benefits to the Commonwealth of the Philippines, to the countries of the Orient, to the peace, prosperity and continued progress that is the hope of the American people.

CLIPPER SIDELIGHTS

By A. G. DAYRIT
Of the Tribune Staff

Flying at a ceiling of 10,000 ft., Pan American's Martin Flying Clipper Ship hove into sight of Manila at 2:50 yesterday afternoon at the end of a course set dead straight from the time it flicked off the last spray from its jaunty tail in the Agana, Guam, harbor at 6:05 (4:05 a. m., Manila time) yesterday morning. At this altitude the China Clipper although already flying over the city, was not visible to Manila's 400,000 as it skimmed above a screening cloud layer. Captain Edwin C. Musick, PAA's keen-eyed ace pilot, eased the ship down to 7,000 ft., and it swam into the ken of expectant tens of thousands. At 2:55, signalling the sighting of the ship 100,000 packed along the bayfront cheered as the sirens and whistles of ships in the bay groaned and shrilled.

* * *

At 7,000 ft. the Clipper, circling leisurely around, looked but like a foot-long silver toy plane to the multitudes gathered below, belying the real size of this third greatest seaplane monster of the world's skyways, this all-metal, highwing 51,000-pound flying boat, powered with four Pratt & Whitney double-row 14-cylinder, 800 h. p. Wasp engines. For fully 30 minutes the Clipper sailed in wide circles over the city, escorted by 16 Army bombing, observation and pursuit planes led by Col. Albert L. Sneed, and five Navy hydroplanes under Lt. Com. Hadden. After having circled around the city for no less than ten times as it gradually reeled in altitude, the Clipper was preened for landing by Captain Musick. As the skybird zoomed low over the Luneta Captain Musick held the throttle back, slowing down the four three bladed controllable pitch propellers, and at 3:30 sharp the black belly of the

(Continued on page 6)

Lands at 3:30 P.M.

Last Leg of Trans-Pacific Flight Negotiated in 11 Hours 22 Minutes

FEAT IS ACCLAIMED

All Manila Wild With Excitement As Giant Plane First Comes to View

By VICENTE J. GUZMAN
Of the Tribune Staff

Manila and its population of 400,000 yesterday afternoon witnessed the making of aviation history as the giant China Clipper, of the Pan American Airways System, [illegible] crossed the vast expanse of the Pacific and landed [illegible] the Manila Bay at [illegible], thus inaugurating the trans-Pacific air mail service between the United States and the Philippines.

Huge Crowd on Hand

The huge metal bird flying a straight route from Guam to Manila, hitherto unexplored, negotiated the distance in 11 hours and 22 minutes. The ship, the largest ever built in America and the third largest seaplane in the world, was accorded the most enthusiastic welcome this city is capable of extending. A crowd estimated at 100,000 was on hand to witness the epochal event.

Plane Slows Down

The last leg of the trans-Pacific crossing, Captain Edwin C. Musick, commander of the China Clipper said, was uneventful. The plane averaged 140 miles an hour during the first half of the Guam-Manila flight but had to slow down the rest of the way in order not to arrive in Manila ahead of schedule.

The clipper hit Manila at an altitude of 10,000 feet. The ship was so high in the air that no one saw it approaching. Captain Musick said the plane circled once around Manila at that altitude and on circling the second time lowered to an altitude of about 7,000 feet.

First Sighted at 2:59

At that altitude, the clipper was first sighted at 2:59 p.m. by thousands who were in the bay on every conceivable water craft and on land to the south of the Manila Bay.

The sight of the white metal sea gull, glimmering in the sun high in the air, its gigantic proportions made more apparent by a swarm of tiny escorts composed of planes of the United States army and navy, thrilled the city's population.

Circles Over Manila

The China Clipper, with Captain Musick and R. O. D. Sullivan, first officer, at the controls, circled at least ten times over Manila for half an hour before it landed. The 400,000 people in the city did not let pass the opportunity of seeing the de luxe air liner during that half-hour period as it flew over Manila.

On the streets, roof tops and windows, parks and plazas, people craned their necks as they looked skyward, following the progress of the flight over the city and the

(Continued on page 7)

GOOD MORNING-JUDGE!

It was merely a case of much too much when Patrolman D. Lucas saw Mr. Maximo Bravo brazenly washing his car on Calle Ongpin, and forthwith arrested him, banishing all his own personal appreciation for the lost art of ablutions which he, however, believes, should be performed, as far as is possible, in strict privacy.

* * *

(1) Chua Kia, (2) Lim King, (3) Chua Pong, (4) Chua Thu, and (5) Sy Chan made ill use of Sy Chan, sent him to a herb doctor after the show was over. This is a symbol of the autonomy move of the five Chinese rebel provinces in obverse.

* * *

In our endless study of racial miscegenation and anthropology we came to the case of Mr. Eutiquio Terry. His last name intrigues us more than the fact that he took one pump, four sockets, 13 ordinary wrenches, and one monkey wrench from Calixto Salonga.

D. R. E. admires the move of the Presiding Speaker in making a gesture to reduce his salary and he approves of it, even if only in principle, but cannot follow suit, as he has almost reached the lowest [illegible] would mean a curtailment of his subscriptions to The Yale Review.

Historic Alameda Flight Recalled

By Victor Wright

It was 30 years ago, on the afternoon of November 22, 1935, that our Pan American Airways China Clipper took off from San Francisco Bay on what was not only the first scheduled transoceanic flight in history but also the first flight across the Pacific to the Orient.

There was a huge crowd to see us off from Alameda on the bay front and there were a lot of speeches about what the flight meant, but I don't think anyone mentioned what was uppermost in the minds of those of us in the crew—that this was also to be the China Clipper's first ocean crossing.

We had made the first four survey flights, during which we had island-hopped as far as Guam, in a smaller flying boat, the S-42. The Martin M-130 or China Clipper, which had been designed and built especially for Pan Am's ocean routes, was a much larger and faster plane with a greater range. We'd picked up this first Clipper at the Baltimore factory and flew her down to Miami, where we made a number of flights so that we could get acquainted with the airplane. Then we ferried her out to San Francisco Bay by flying across the Gulf of Mexico and the narrow part of Mexico at the Isthmus of Tehuantepec (as the Clipper was a flying boat, we had to stay as close as we could to water) and then up through Acapulco and San Diego to San Francisco.

No Time for Bunk

After the S-42, the China Clipper seemed pretty big to us. The hull of the Clipper was 90 feet from bow to stern, from the pilots' compartment to the after end of the cabin. Since we would be carrying no paying passengers on the early trips, they'd stripped the seats and furnishings out of the cabin to make room for mail and cargo. So there was plenty of room to move around in but no place where you could make yourself really comfortable. But that didn't bother us because we knew that with a new plane and a new ocean to fly, we'd be too busy to do much resting. As a matter of fact, we had a bunk up forward, but I don't remember anyone using it.

Our departure from Alameda was spectacular, though we didn't plan it that way. After leaving the waterfront ramp Captain Edwin C. Musick circled on the water a few times to warm up the engines and then headed up the bay toward the looping wires of the San Francisco-Oakland bridge, then being built. As we left the water a convoy of escorting planes closed in behind us.

It had been our intention to fly over the bridge, but Musick quickly saw that with the engine cowl flaps open he wouldn't be able to get up enough speed to clear the wires, so he nosed the Clipper down at the last moment and went under the bridge cables, threading his way through the dangling construction wires. We all ducked and held our breaths until we were in the clear. I think the little planes must have been as surprised as we were, but they all followed us right through.

For that first leg of the trip—the long, overnight hop to Honolulu—there were just us seven crew members aboard the China Clipper. There were two pilots, plane commander Musick and R.O.D. Sullivan, two engineers, both of us named Wright but unrelated, navigators Fred Noonan and George King and radio operator Wilson T. Jarboe, Jr. Each of us was trained for more than one job, so that we could spell one another during long flights. For example, though I was primarily an engineering officer at that time, I also held a transport pilot's license and a radio operator's certificate, so I could fill in at those posts.

With no passengers, we could dress for comfort on the flight to Hawaii. As soon as we'd cleared the coast we got out of the uniforms we'd worn for the departure ceremonies and put on something comfortable, as they say, for the 21-hour flight which lay ahead. I wore a pair of red pajamas and bedroom slippers, I remember, and the rest of the crew were just about as informal. We were a strange-looking bunch of trailblazers.

Walked Across Ocean

In those days we didn't have all the instruments and the cockpit indicators they now use and the engineer had to roam around the Clipper, spot-checking the various control systems. And whenever the navigator needed a hand, one of us would have to go back to the after-end of the cabin and check on our drift by sighting on the flares he had released. Then there were frequent fuel checks and conferences with the plane commander, as we were always trying to get as many miles as possible out of the engines for the fuel we used.

All this kept me moving around from one end of the Clipper to the other during that long night flight to Honolulu. I walked through the dawn, which caught us by the tail, and had breakfast from the sandwiches I carried in a paper bag. And I was still walking when the peaks of Hawaii rose out of a cloud bank in the west. (And I was still walking when we raised the Philippines. I often claim I'm the only man who ever walked across the Pacific.)

By that time we'd been out almost 20 hours and even the non-walkers were feeling a little weary. And then Captain Musick surprised us. We were told to shave (in cold water, at that) and get back into uniform. There was some grumbling, but we realized later that this was a master stroke. Getting cleaned up not only made us feel better—when the crew stepped off the Clipper all spic and span you'd thought we'd just taken a swing around the harbor. It made the ocean crossing look routine.

There was an official reception at Honolulu, but it was small scale. We'd been through Hawaii on four survey flights and flying the Pacific was getting to be old hat to the people there. But the welcoming committee and all our Navy friends seemed to be impressed with our carefully creased uniforms and our white caps and our bright and shining faces. There were some speeches and they handed out leis. All I wanted by that time was a place to sit down.

First Passengers

That night at Honolulu we loaded up with a lot of food and equipment for the island bases. And we took on 14 company passengers, replacements for the ground staffs on the islands. We could do that because the flight to Midway was only about half the distance of the San Francisco to Honolulu hop, so we carried less gas. And the navigation on this leg was simple. It was a daylight flight and we followed a curving chain of reefs and islands, covering the 1,380 miles in 8½ hours.

During the survey flights we had enjoyed our layover time at Midway—fishing, swimming and teaching the gooney birds to fly by holding them over our heads and racing down the beach. On this trip, with a new type of plane, we were kept busy checking over the Clipper and taking the island maintenance crews on conducted tours of the ship. All this had to be done with the Clipper floating out in the lagoon.

On the way to Wake Island the next day we passed two "signposts" on an otherwise lonely and vacant ocean. The first was the International Dateline, which added a day to our schedule. This produced an interesting situation toward the end of the trip. A second passage occurred when we overflew the Matson liner, the President Lincoln, which was on its way to Japan. This gave us a welcome chance to check our navigation, for which we used dead reckoning, shots of the sun and the island-based radio direction finders which kept a constant watch over the flight. We were on course—as we had to be for this leg, for Wake Island was just a pinpoint surrounded by the vast Pacific. Actually, our flight went so well that we landed on the lagoon at Wake five minutes ahead of schedule.

Opened Clipper's Windows

Our flight to Guam the next day was a somewhat longer duplicate of the Midway-Wake Island hop. We tried various altitudes (the Clipper performed best at about 8,000 feet) to make the most of the trade winds which were now pushing us along. As an indication of how flying has changed—at 1,200 feet we found it so warm and comfortable that we opened all the windows.

We had a little trick for getting additional radio bearings as we approached Guam. There was a Japanese radio station on Rota, an island about 50 miles north of Guam, and when we were about an hour out of Apra Harbor we'd send out a CQ or "Do you hear me?" signal on the Japanese frequency. Then, while he was answering our call, we'd get a bearing on his station on Guam to get a good fix on our position. We couldn't use that one too often, though, because in 1935 the Japanese weren't interested in helping anyone establish an airline across the Pacific.

Everybody in Guam seemed to have turned out to give us a welcome. This was just as well, because after we'd landed we discovered that someone in Manila who had scheduled the arrival celebration had apparently been confused by the time changes caused by the International Dateline and had provided us with an extra day of flying time. This meant that if we continued our flight the next morning we would arrive in Manila a day before they were ready to greet us. So we laid over a day on Guam and tried to make ourselves as inconspicuous as possible. That wasn't too easy with people all around the world watching the news of the flight and wondering where you are. We solved that by simply closing down the radio for everything but essential communications.

The Guam to Manila leg of the flight introduced a new note, for this was the first time anyone had flown across that particular stretch of ocean. But we were so sure of ourselves by this time—of the China Clipper and our flight procedures and the communications network that guarded us along the way—that we just took it in stride. There was a stir aboard when we raised the volcanic cone of Mount Mayan from 11,000 feet and 150 miles out, but that was chiefly because that meant it was time to clean up and get back into uniform for the welcoming celebration at Manila.

They gave us a great reception at Manila. I particularly enjoyed the official banquet and the automobile tour around the city, because I could take them both sitting down. They gave us each several sheets of first-flight stamps commemorating the first mail flight across the Pacific and I managed to get hold of the flag we flew at the China Clipper's bow as we taxied in to our mooring. I still have both the stamps and the flags as souvenirs of the first commercial flight across the Pacific—and the memory of a pair of aching feet.

(Taken from the *Alameda Times Star*, Nov. 17, 1965.)

Victor Wright, flight engineer on the initial flights of the S-42 and M-130. He later was promoted to captain.   PAA

Wilson T. Jarboe, Jr., flight radio officer on the initial flights of the S-42 and M-130 and a long-time employee of Pan Am.   PAA

Capt. Victor Wright at the Miami airport (1965) holding the flag that was carried on the *China Clipper* flight to Manila in 1935.   PAA

FIRST PASSENGER FLIGHT

Within a year, Pan Am began scheduled passenger service to Manila. Before regular flights could begin, however, the airline had to see to it that the clippers were ready and able to withstand the rigors of a regular schedule. In addition, Pan Am had to complete facilities for passengers in the islands. The demand for passenger service was proving greater than anticipated, and Pan Am had advanced construction deadlines by many months.

No hotels needed to be built for passengers staying over in Manila and Hawaii. But on Guam, an existing facility required extensive work before it would be ready to house clipper passengers. And on Wake, and Midway, in order to provide clipper passengers with suitable overnight accommodations, Pan Am had to start from scratch.

Two complete, prefabricated hotels, each containing 45 rooms, were loaded aboard the *North Haven* in January of 1936. Destined for Wake and Midway, these hotels had been designed with tropical conditions in mind. Of frame construction, each consisted of two wings with a central circular lobby, and boasted of a shower bath with hot water in every room.

Everything needed to furnish a modern hotel soon found itself loaded aboard the *North Haven:* furniture for bedrooms and social rooms, right down to ashtrays and coat hangers; cashiers' cages; inter-room telephones; desks, and draperies. On the islands, workers built tennis courts and swimming pools. Aquariums were stocked with native tropical fish, and staffs of service personnel were hired who could be counted on to provide guests with red-carpet treatment.

Over a thousand would-be passengers had applied for seven seats on the inaugural flight scheduled for Oct. 21, 1936. A flight aboard the *Hawaii Clipper* with Capt. Musick in command would not be cheap. A passenger traveling only as far as Hawaii had to pay $360, while a one-way ticket from San Francisco to Manila cost nearly $800.

The first passenger flight lifted off the water at Alameda on Oct. 21, 1936, at 2:59 p.m. One passenger disembarked in Honolulu, where an additional five passengers boarded the clipper for Manila. The six-day flight occurred without incident, as did the return flight, which landed at San Francisco on Nov. 11.

Seven passengers made the inaugural flight to Hawaii on Oct. 22, 1936, in the *Hawaii Clipper*. Posing here at Alameda, they are (left to right): R.F. Bradley, aviation manager of Standard Oil of California; Wilbur May, Los Angeles department store executive; Mrs. Clara Adams of Stroudsburg, Pa.; Cole Charles Bartley, owner of a large Chicago grocery firm; T.F. Ryan III, San Francisco industrialist; Alfred Bennett, an aviation executive; and Mrs. Zetta Averill of Aberdeen, Wash. The women in the photo are listed as "World Travelers."   PAA

Crew and mechanics line up next to the plane while Patricia Kennedy, in the bow, pours coconut milk over the Clipper as a symbol of good luck.   HA

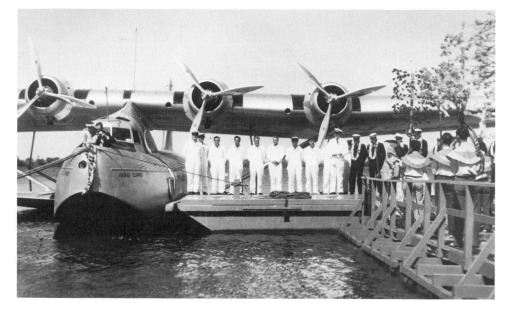

The *Hawaii Clipper* on the water at Ford Island, Pearl Harbor, after completing the first leg of the first passenger flight.   PAA

As with all the first flights, the crew and passengers are feted to a royal welcome upon arrival in Hawaii on Oct. 22.
PAA

Capt. Musick is welcomed to Hawaii once again.   PAA

The first trans-Pacific passengers board the *Hawaii Clipper* at Honolulu to continue their flight to Manila. The *China Clipper* lies in the background, ready to head back to San Francisco.   HA

Mrs. Clara Adams with Mr. Louis Weinzheimer at the Cavite terminal on Oct. 31, just before her departure on the first eastbound passenger flight.   PAA

Crew members Weber, Noonan and Musick disembark the *Hawaii Clipper* on Oct. 27, shortly after having completed the first passenger flight across the Pacific.   PAA

More "first flights" were in the offing, some dramatic, others routine. The *China Clipper* actually preceded her sister's first passenger flight with a round-trip press flight to Manila from Oct. 7 to 24. The *Philippine Clipper* carried a plane load of officials and the press to Manila, then continued on to make the first clipper flight to Hong Kong on Oct. 23, 1936, with Mr. and Mrs. Juan Trippe aboard on their first round-the-world journey.

First flights became almost commonplace in the months to come:

March 17, 1937. In an S-42B, Capt. Musick began the first South Pacific survey flight from San Francisco to Auckland, New Zealand, via Honolulu, Pago Pago, American Samoa, and Kingman Reef.

April 21, 1937. The first airmail flight from San Francisco to Hong Kong via Macao made use of two planes, the *China Clipper* (San Francisco—Manila) and the S-42 *Hong Kong Clipper* (Manila to Macao and Hong Kong). This journey marked the first clipper flight to Macao on April 28.

May 5, 1937. An M-130 and an S-42 combined to make the first scheduled passenger flight to Hong Kong.

Dec. 23, 1937. Captain Musick left San Francisco on a second survey flight to Auckland aboard the S-42B *Samoan Clipper.*

Feb. 5, 1939. The *China Clipper* made the first flight from Pan Am's new base at Treasure Island in San Francisco Bay.

Feb. 22, 1939. The first flight of the new B-314 flying boat, the *California Clipper,* began at Treasure Island.

Nov. 30, 1939. A B-314, the *Honolulu Clipper* completed a 16,000-mile familiarization flight to Auckland, New Zealand, and back, under the command of Capt. W.A. Cluthe, following the first B-314 survey flight along the same route in August.

June 24, 1940. Service was extended from San Francisco to Los Angeles to Honolulu.

July 12, 1940. A B-314 made the first regular airmail run from San Francisco to New Zealand via a new route: Los Angeles, Honolulu, Canton Island and Noumea, New Caledonia. On Sept. 11, passenger service began over this route.

July 23, 1940. Direct service began from Honolulu to Los Angeles.

May 2, 1941. B-314s inaugurated bi-weekly airmail service from San Francisco to Singapore via Manila, soon followed by regular passenger service.

Aug. 10, 1941. Daily B-314 service began between San Francisco and Honolulu.

Nov. 5, 1941. The final trail to be blazed before the outbreak of war in the Pacific provided passenger service from San Francisco to New Zealand via Los Angeles, Honolulu, Canton Island, Suva in the Fiji Islands, and Noumea, New Caledonia.

Following the outbreak of World War II, four years would pass, during which Pacific skies would be far too dangerous for commercial flights. On Nov. 16, 1945, commercial flights to Honolulu were re-inaugurated, but the era of the flying boat had all but ended. By early 1946, commercial aviation relied solely upon more advanced, land-based airplanes.

Inauguration of a B-314 flight.　　　　PAA

B-314 #NC-18605 at San Diego, 1946. All the 314s were scrapped or sunk in the ocean by the early 1950s.   PAA

CHAPTER TWELVE

END OF AN ERA:
THE LEGACY OF THE CLIPPERS

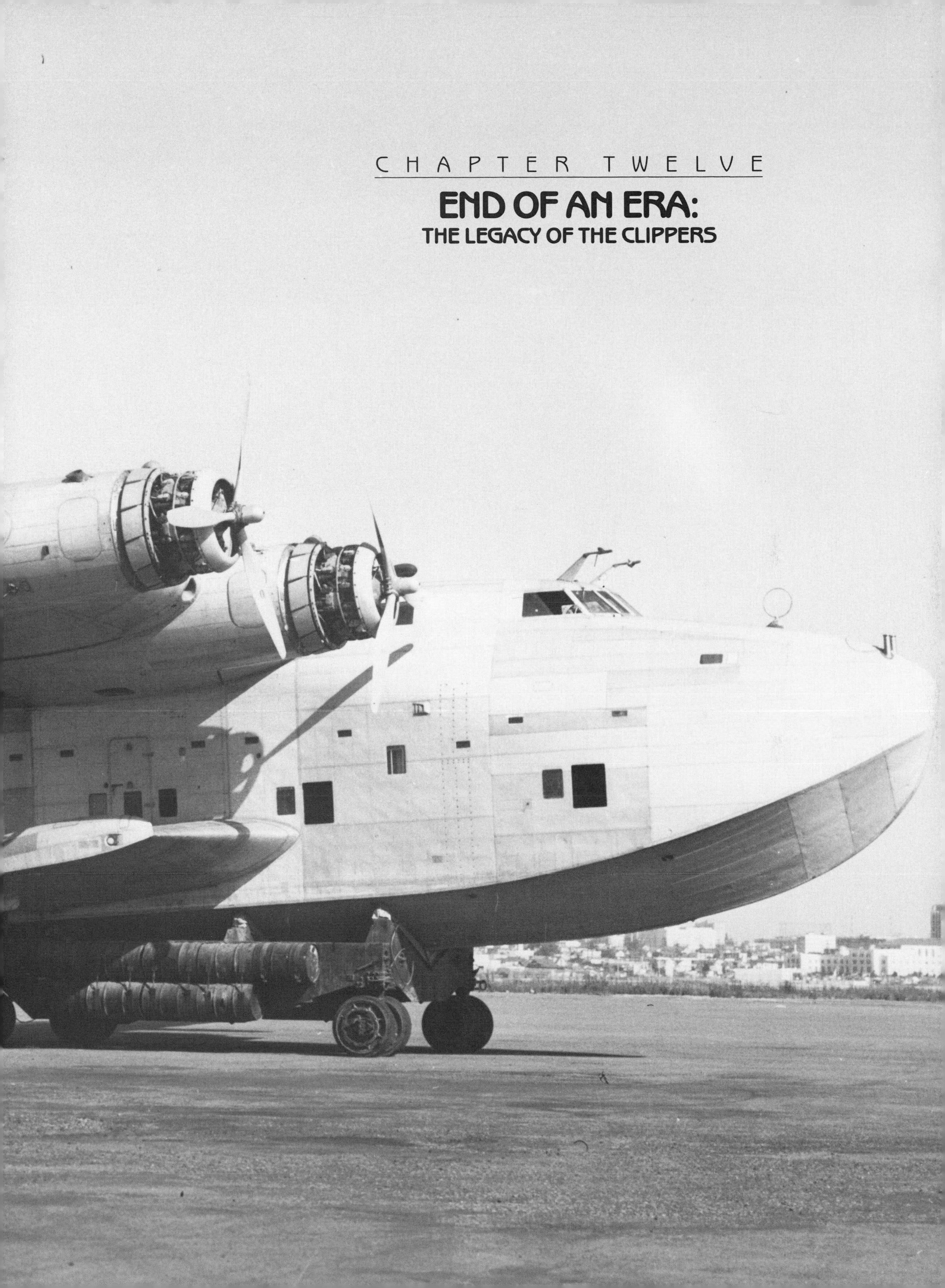

END OF AN ERA

Pan Am's commercial flying-boat era came to an abrupt end on the fateful morning of Dec. 7, 1941, when the Japanese delivered a devastating blow to the U.S. Fleet at Pearl Harbor and attacked bases at Midway, Wake, Guam, the Philippines and Hong Kong. What the Japanese had not been able to do in the 1930s—stop the trans-Pacific flights by sabotage and intimidation—they were able to accomplish by force of arms.

War clouds had been gathering in the Pacific for years, as the Japanese eyed the Dutch East Indies, the Philippines and south and central Pacific islands with a mind toward expansion. Pan Am recognized the threat inherent in the Japanese vision of a Greater East-Asia Co-Prosperity Sphere. By August 1939, the airline had painted American flags on the bows and wings of all the Clippers as a precaution against inadvertent attack by Japanese aircraft.

Four Clippers were in the air or on the water at Pan Am's forward bases on that now-famous Sunday morning, (Monday morning west of the dateline). The *China Clipper* had recently returned from Manila. She alone lay safe in San Francisco Bay the day of the attack. The *Hawaii Clipper* had been lost in the Pacific in 1938, or might easily have been a casualty at Pearl Harbor.

The *Anzac Clipper*, a B-314, was just an hour away from Pearl Harbor when the Japanese attacked. As was true on all the Clippers, the *Anzac Clipper's* pilot carried sealed orders that were to be opened in the case of such an attack.* Following these new, wartime instructions, the Clipper's crew proceeded to Hilo on the big island of Hawaii, trusting to luck that they would not encounter the Japanese Fleet or its aircraft. Within two hours Capt. H. Lanier Turner had reached Hilo, unloaded passengers and mail, and refueled by hand. The *Anzac Clipper* returned to San Francisco, leaving Hilo at night to avoid the possibility of Japanese daytime patrols.

The *Philippine Clipper*, with 34-year-old Capt. John Hamilton at the controls, had just left Wake on a routine flight to Guam, carrying a military mission, a Flying Tigers pilot and a cargo of airplane tires, all destined for China. As word reached Wake of the Pearl

---
*Orders were to fly the plane to the nearest safe port and to insure the safety of the passengers and the mail if possible.

Harbor attack, Capt. Hamilton was called back. Wake's two commanders, Comdr. W.S. Cunningham and Maj. James Devereaux, requested that Hamilton's plane be used to escort the Marine Corps F4F fighter planes on patrol around the island.

But such a patrol was not to take place. At approximately 9:30 a.m., on December 8 (Wake time), 36 Japanese bombers roared over the island. The bombers had flown in from Kwajalein, 600 miles to the south, and due to the noise of the surf, had arrived undetected. They destroyed the airfield and seven of the Marine F4F fighters, along with fuel depots and buildings. Twenty-three squadron members were killed.

The Clipper, strafed at her dock, suffered more than 60 bullet holes yet somehow avoided a disabling hit. Ten Chamorro (natives of Guam) airline personnel were killed, and most of the Pan Am facilities, including the direction finder and hotel, were destroyed. Capt. Hamilton had no way of knowing if the D.F. on Midway, or if any of Midway's Pan Am facilities, remained intact. Yet there was no doubt in his mind that an immediate evacuation of Pan Am personnel was imperative.

The *Philippine Clipper* was stripped of her mail and cargo to make room for 70 Pan Am employees to board her for the trip east. Hamilton approached Midway without the aid of the island's direction finder, as Midway, too, had been bombed by the Japanese. The Clipper's crew guided her to a safe landing in part through the visual aid presented by the large number of fires on the island. An hour after landing on Midway, the *Philippine Clipper* was once again airborne, this time for Hawaii and Pan Am's undamaged base at Pearl City. Shortly before landing, she passed over the unforgettable scene of destruction at Pearl Harbor.

Midway saw more than one attack by Japanese forces. On December 7, at 9:30 p.m., two cruisers and two destroyers from the Japanese Pearl Harbor raiding force attacked the island. Four U.S. military personnel were killed, and Pan Am's facilities were damaged; however, Pan Am's employees on Midway escaped injury. Six months later, on June 4, 1942, the majority of aboveground facilities, including those of Pan Am, were destroyed during the Battle of Midway.

Nor was Guam so fortunate as to escape the first day of the war. Guam, which had long been sur-

CIVILIAN INTERNEES

In December of 1941, at the outbreak of the war in the Pacific, 12 American and 32 Chamorro employees of Pan American were captured on Wake and Guam. All of the Americans survived nearly four years of confinement in prisoner of war camps in Japan.

After the initial attack on Wake (Dec. 8, Wake time), Pan Am personnel were assembled for evacuation, with the exception of Waldo Ranquist. Ranquist, who was driving the wounded to a first aid station, sent word with one of his fellow workers that the Clipper should leave without him if he did not get to the dock in time for the plane's scheduled departure. As a result of his altruism, Ranquist would spend the next four years in Japan with other civilian contractors and Wake Island marines. He would not be heard from until August 1945, when a telegram would arrive in Pan Am's office in San Francisco with the following message: "Have been liberated. Am now in Manila. Received money order yes-terday.[Pan Am had sent a check for $100 to buy incidentals before returning home.] Will be back soon. Waldo Ranquist."

Eleven American employees were captured on Guam while attempting to hide in the hills.* Charles Gregg, airport manager, acted as the leader of the group, both on Guam and later in the POW camp. The men captured on Guam were taken to the capital, Agana. After 30 days, they were transported to Japan for internment in Zentsuji Prison on Shikoku Island, and later taken to Kobe where they would remain until the end of the war.

On April 18, 1942, Pan Am employees held prisoner in Japanese camps witnessed Doolittle's raid on Tokyo. And beginning in 1945, they had an unenviable view of American B-29 bombing raids. To a man, they survived the harshness of prison life and were found to be in reasonably good health when liberated in September of 1945.

*Richard Arvidson, Fred Oppenborn, George Blackett, Max Brodofsky, George Conklin, Charles Gregg, Alfred Hammeley, Everett Penning, James Thomas, Robert Vaughn, Grant Wells.

The *China Clipper* in its wartime colors.

PAA

rounded by Japanese controlled islands, was in easy range of land-based Japanese bombers. At 8:45 a.m. on December 8 (Guam time), the Japanese attacked Guam, bombing the radio station and the island's fuel tanks, and sinking the minesweeper U.S.S. *Penguin* in Apra Harbor. Within days, Japanese troops had overwhelmed the tiny U.S. garrison of Marines and the island surrendered.

Pan Am's base in the Philippines, Cavite, was also lost in the early days of the war. On December 8 Japanese bombers flying in from Formosa caught the U.S. Army's planes on the ground at Clark Field, inflicting a disabling blow to the islands' defenses. Pan Am officials destroyed the base prior to Japanese occupation. Thirty-three employees were eventually captured and spent the war in internment camps. Hong Kong shared the fate of the rest of the trans-Pacific system. Here, the *Hong Kong Clipper* lay tied at her dock at Kai-tak Airport on the Kowloon Peninsula. Eight DC-2s and DC-3s belonging to Pan Am's affiliate, CNAC, were parked on the runway.

Upon hearing of the attack on Pearl Harbor, the man in charge of Pan Am's interest in CNAC, William Langhorne Bond, ordered the *Hong Kong Clipper* to leave Hong Kong for an island lake near Kunming, China. But before the plane could be readied for departure, Japanese bombers passed over the city, unloading their payload on the airport's runways, and setting the clipper on fire. CNAC lost five planes and the *Hong Kong Clipper* burned to water level.

In the next few days Bond gathered Pan Am personnel and a number of Chinese civilians and evacuated them to China. On December 12, Hong Kong fell to the Japanese, but not before Bond had managed to evacuate 275 people, three aircraft and their crews, and a supply of spare parts.

As Portugal remained neutral during the war, the Portuguese colony of Macao was not occupied by Japanese troops, and Pan Am's facilities remained intact. Ironically, the Pan Am base at Macao would be destroyed by U.S. bombers. The Allies did not want Pan Am's supply of precious aviation fuel to fall into the hands of the enemy. On January 16, 1945, in spite of the neutrality of Macao, the tanks and other airline facilities were destroyed. They were never to be used again.

With the exception of Macao and Honolulu, all of Pan Am's Pacific outposts were under Japanese occupation by the end of December 1941. Trippe's airline entered into wartime service. Nine B-314s and two M-130s were stripped of prewar refinements and painted a dull sea gray.

The two remaining Martin flying boats were turned over to the Navy in 1942, although they continued to be flown by Pan Am crews. In 1943, both were again placed under the control of Pan Am and employed in a shuttle service between San Francisco and Honolulu. Neither would survive the war.

After 14,628 hours in the air, having survived 60 bullet holes from the strafing of a Japanese bomber at Wake, the *Philippine Clipper* ended her service a few miles west of Ukiah, California, the morning of Jan. 21, 1943. Nine crewmen and 10 Navy passengers were killed as the gallant plane, due to bad weather and possible navigational errors, crashed into the side of a mountain.

The last of the Martin flying boats, the *China Clipper*, continued the San Francisco-Honolulu shuttle until June 1943, when she was transferred to Florida to begin a shuttle from Miami to Leopoldville in the Belgian Congo. She, too, met a tragic end, hitting an unidentified object in the water at Port of Spain, Trinidad, on Jan. 8, 1945. Nine of 12 crew members and 14 of 18 passengers died in the crash.

Nine B-314s entered military service following Pearl Harbor. They continued flying under Pan Am crews, transporting cargo and military personnel across the Atlantic to Africa and India, including among their passengers the commander-in-chief, President Roosevelt, and his staff. One of these planes crashed during the war, and most that survived were scrapped in 1946.

POST WAR OPERATIONS

After the war, plans to operate the flying boats over both the Atlantic and Pacific routes were soon canceled in favor of the new, land-based DC-4. Jan. 6, 1946, marked the end of B-314 service across the Pacific. Commercial shuttle flights between California and Hawaii had resumed in November of 1945, but they, too, were discontinued on April 8, 1946.

World Airways flew several B-314s for charter service, Puerto Rico-New York, in the late 1940s. They were scrapped in the early 1950s.

The last flight of a Pacific Pan Am Clipper took place on April 8-9, 1946, when a B-314, *American Clipper*, NC-18606, took off from Honolulu for Mills Field, San Francisco. The last Alantic flight was on Dec. 24, 1945.

The era of the Clippers was over even more quickly than it had begun. Today, nothing remains of the three Martin 130s, not even a section of a broken wing on display at an aviation museum. Of twelve B-314s that saw service, there are but a few pieces of NC 18602, which can be seen at the Pacific Museum of Flight in Seattle, Wash. Several models of M-130s and B-314s, on display at aviation museums and archives around the country, are all that is left for the student of aviation history.

AN INCREDIBLE JOURNEY

On the morning of Jan. 6, 1942, at 7:12, the *Pacific Clipper* landed unheralded at the La Guardia Field seaplane base after a history-making journey. While in the air between New Caledonia and Auckland, on a routine flight between Honolulu and New Zealand, this Boeing 314 had received word that the Japanese had bombed Pearl Harbor. Capt. Robert Ford and his crew (First Officers John Henry Mack, Second Officer Norman Brown, Third Officer James G. Henriksen, Fourth Officer John Delmer Steers, First Engineer Homans K. Rothe, Second Engineer John Bertrand Parish, First Radio Officer John D. Poindexter, Second Radio Officer Oscar Hendrickson, Flight Steward Barney Sawicki and Assistant Flight Steward Verne C. Edwards) landed at Auckland and awaited orders from New York headquarters.

Ford knew that the way back to San Francisco now lay under Japanese threat. Yet he must have been surprised when he received orders to fly "the long way round" from Auckland to New York, a feat that had never before been attempted by a commercial aircraft.

The flight, which was to take 25 days, set a number of aviation records: the first aerial crossing between New Caledonia and Australia; the first round-the-world flight by a commercial plane; the longest continuous trip ever made by a commercial plane; and the first round-the-world flight by a plane following a route near the equator. In addition, the Clipper flew thousands of miles *over land* while crossing Australia, Arabia and Africa, an extremely dangerous journey for a flying boat. Her 3,583-mile journey from West Africa to South America, was the longest nonstop flight in Pan Am's history. And more than 8,500 miles of this incredible Auckland-to-San Francisco journey were logged over territory new to Pan Am pilots. Total mileage flown from San Francisco to New York was 31,500.

Portions of the route were flown without advanced weather reports, or sea bases where the Clipper could be serviced. The flight was unequaled as a test of ingenuity, self-reliance and resourcefulness. At a number of stops along the way, aviation fuel was not available, requiring that the plane make do with regular automobile gasoline. Repair facilities were unavailable, as were the specialized tools needed to work on the clipper. At Trincomalee, Ceylon, a special tool needed to replace the studs on an engine cylinder was discovered to have been left behind in New Zealand. Undaunted, the second engineering officer visited a British warship anchored in the harbor, borrowing a piece of steel and a lathe, and making a duplicate tool. Perhaps it was fitting that the British should come to the aid of the Clipper, after an earlier incident over the Dutch East Indies when British fighter planes came close to shooting her down.

Before beginning his trip west, Capt. Ford had to backtrack to New Caledonia and pick up Pan Am personnel waiting to fly to Australia. After landing in Gladstone, Australia, the *Pacific Clipper* proceeded to fly to Darwin in northern Australia, Surabaya (Dutch East Indies), Trincomalee (Ceylon), Karachi (India), Bahrein (Arabia), Khartoum (Anglo-Egyptian Sudan), Leopoldville (Belgian Congo), and then across the South Atlantic to Belem (Brazil). From Brazil, the final leg of the Clipper's journey took her to Trinidad, Puerto Rico and New York.

It was an audacious journey, but Ford and his crew had made it without any major incidents, bringing a much-needed Clipper home for use in the war effort.

SAN FRANCISCO
APR 23
4 PM
CALIF
1935

UNITED STATES POSTAGE
WASHINGTON
3 CENTS

FROM

Pan American Airways, Inc.,

HONOLULU, H. T., U. S. A.

FIRST FLIGHT
PAN AMERICAN CLIPPER
HAWAII·CALIFORNIA

POSTAL HISTORY

During the 1930s and early 1940s, the Pan American Airways System provided postal history buffs and stamp collectors with an unusual opportunity to collect first flight covers. The four survey flights, the first airmail flight (1935), final inspection trip (1936), first passenger flight (1936), first flights of the B-314 (1939) and the several legs of the trans-Pacific route, both east and west, were subjects of individual stamps marking the importance of these first flights.

The first S-42 survey flight (Alameda to Hawaii, April 16, 1935) was not a scheduled airmail run. However, the Post Office Department authorized mail to be carried on the flight at domestic airmail rates—six cents per leg. Letters returning to California required additional postage in order to be forwarded to their mainland destinations.

At the time of the second S-42 survey flight, there were no postal facilities on the island of Midway. Although it was as yet impossible for any first covers to receive a Midway postmark, the crew of the S-42 hand carried an unknown quantity of these covers, posting them in Honolulu. The first flight covers from these two survey flights were not permitted to contain letters or other regular correspondence. They were intended solely as a unique opportunity for the collector.

The *China Clipper*'s inaugural flight (Alameda to Manila, Nov. 29, 1935) provided the public with its first chance to send a letter to the Orient via airmail. The Clipper carried 58 bags of mail weighing 1837 pounds and totalling 110,865 letters: 46,561 for Honolulu, 19,958 for Guam, and 44,346 for Manila. A total of 206,414 stamps were sold and would be cancelled with the distinctive cachets designed by Pan Am personnel at the individual stops along the trans-Pacific route. The most-prized, first-day issues were signed by the Clipper's crew members.

J.H. Underwood, postmaster at Guam at the time of the first survey flight, recounts the magnitude of interest in these first covers:

"My greatest interest was in the 'First Flight' mail for Guam, how much there was of it and how it was to be handled. I was directed to the Assistant Navigator, Mr. H.N. Canaday, and arrangements were made for the transportation of the bags of mail to the Post Office at Agana, 12 miles distant, and for the postmarking with the date and hour of arrival. . . . As mail of this class had never been handled in the Guam office before, the preliminary work was done under the direct instructions and observance of Mr. Canaday, the officer in charge of this mail. Every effort was made to make a clear and legible impression of the post mark on each cover, or envelope, and in the proper place. The incoming letters were divided into six classes, and the number of pieces and weight of each class was recorded separately. They were: letters from San Francisco to Guam to San Francisco—round trip; letters from Honolulu to Guam to Honolulu—round trip; letters from San Francisco to Guam to be returned to San Francisco by ordinary mail and by air mail from San Francisco to destinations in the United States if other than San Francisco; San Francisco to Guam to Honolulu; Honolulu to Guam to San Francisco; and San Francisco to Guam—final destination, i.e. letters addressed to residents of Guam. In addition to the above six classes, there were: letters from Guam to Honolulu; and letters from Guam to San Francisco. The total number of letters handled was about 6400. The greater part of these had to be held in the Post Office and stamped again with the date of sailing of the Clipper Ship from Guam on her return to San Francisco, 5:00 a.m., Wednesday, 16 October, 1935. As there was only one postmarking stamp in the Post Office, a steel hand stamp, we had to take turns in doing the work, as one's arm became almost paralyzed after a thousand or more blows with the stamp, and these 'blows' had to be carefully spaced and graduated in force in order not to spoil any of the covers. Of course some of the larger Post Offices will smile at the idea of handling 6400 letters in one day, but when it is considered that this office has only *one* regular clerk, and *one* piece of equipment for handling this quantity, it will be realized that the job was not so insignificant as it might appear at first sight. Consider too that the Postmaster and his one assistant are not accustomed to or have not had the experience and training that come from handling large quantities of mail regularly. I regret that I did not have time to observe the names of the persons to whom these letters were addressed, as this would have been of considerable interest. However, in the hurry of getting this work done properly, it was noted that there were covers addressed to His Holiness Pope Pius XI, President Franklin D. Roosevelt, Postmaster General James E. Farley, and other State Officials, many 'Movie' Stars, and dozens of Stamp Collectors whose names are known to the Postmaster from previous correspondence with them."*

*From *The Guam Recorder,* November 1935, Number 140

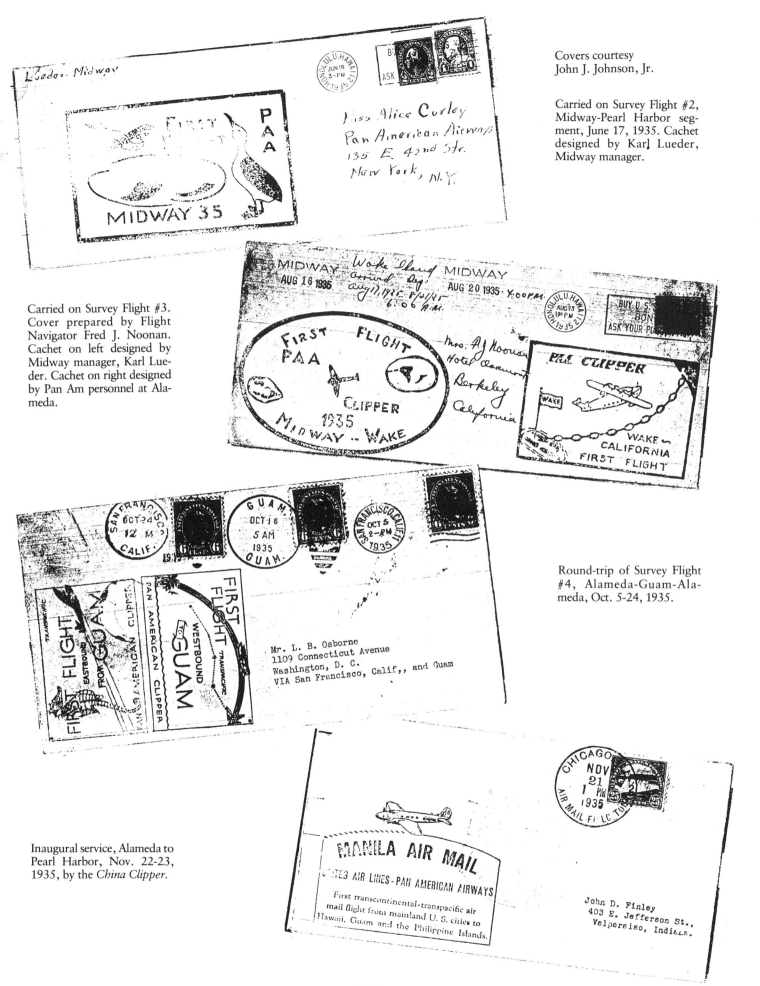

Covers courtesy
John J. Johnson, Jr.

Carried on Survey Flight #2,
Midway-Pearl Harbor seg-
ment, June 17, 1935. Cachet
designed by Karl Lueder,
Midway manager.

Carried on Survey Flight #3.
Cover prepared by Flight
Navigator Fred J. Noonan.
Cachet on left designed by
Midway manager, Karl Lue-
der. Cachet on right designed
by Pan Am personnel at Ala-
meda.

Round-trip of Survey Flight
#4, Alameda-Guam-Ala-
meda, Oct. 5-24, 1935.

Inaugural service, Alameda to
Pearl Harbor, Nov. 22-23,
1935, by the *China Clipper.*

First airmail flight, Hawaii-San Francisco, Dec. 5-6, 1935.

Public relations flight of the *Philippines Clipper,* Oct. 14 to Nov. 2, 1936, on the Alameda-Guam segment, Oct. 14-19, 1936. Signed by flight commander Capt. J.H. Tilton.

Inaugural flight, B-314, NC-18602, the *California Clipper,* March 6-11, 1939, San Francisco to Hong Kong and return.

Macao-Guam, 1937.

Hong Kong to Pearl Harbor.
Crew signed.

Mailed at Midway and carried in the pilot's pouch to Wake, Guam, then back to Wake, Midway and Pearl Harbor, where it entered the regular U.S. mail system, April 25, 1939.

Clipper mail, Hawaii-San Francisco. Posted on the USS *West Virginia*, September 1941. The ship was based at Pearl Harbor.

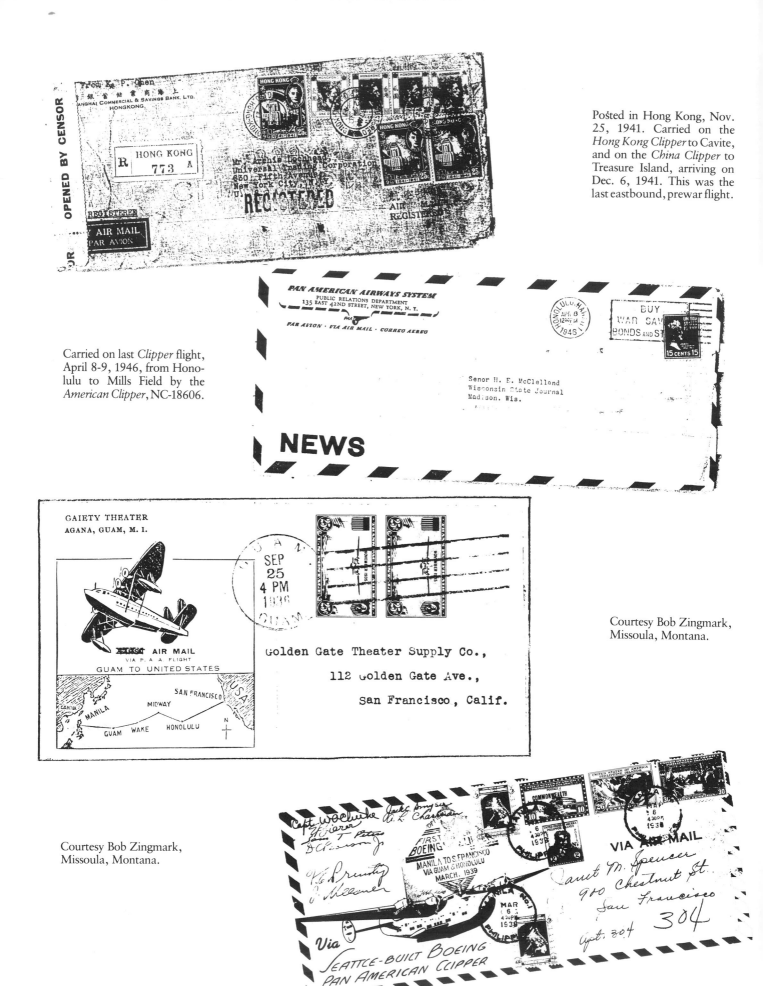

Posted in Hong Kong, Nov. 25, 1941. Carried on the *Hong Kong Clipper* to Cavite, and on the *China Clipper* to Treasure Island, arriving on Dec. 6, 1941. This was the last eastbound, prewar flight.

Carried on last *Clipper* flight, April 8-9, 1946, from Honolulu to Mills Field by the *American Clipper*, NC-18606.

Courtesy Bob Zingmark, Missoula, Montana.

Courtesy Bob Zingmark, Missoula, Montana.

APPENDIX

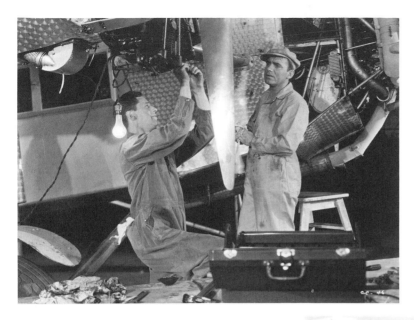

The 1936 motion picture *China Clipper* starred Pat O'Brien, Humphrey Bogart, Ross Alexander and Beverly Roberts. Produced by First National Productions Corporation, this movie was the first aviation feature to be made without a flight-related loss of life. The *China Clipper* flying boat appeared in several of the film's sequences.

Author's Collection

Pan American's family of clippers on display at the Pacific Museum of Flight in Seattle.

Sheet music from the 1930s.   PAA

FIRST FLIGHTS

TRANSPACIFIC SURVEY FLIGHT 1935
NUMBER 1

San Francisco, California—Honolulu, Hawaii

Lv. San Francisco (Alameda) . . . 6:50 p.m. EST, April 16
Ar. Honolulu (Pearl Harbor) . . 12:59 p.m. EST, April 17

18 hrs., 9 mins.
Air Miles—2,301

Lv. Honolulu . . . . 8:59 p.m. EST, April 22
Ar. San Francisco . . . . 5:59 p.m. EST, April 23

20 hrs., 59 mins.
Air Miles—2,740

CREW: Captain Edwin C. Musick
      1st Officer R.O.D. Sullivan
      Engineering Officer V.A. Wright
      Jr. Flight Officer H.R. Canaday
      Navigation Officer F.J. Noonan
      Radio Officer W.T. Jarboe, Jr.

AIRCRAFT: Sikorsky S-42
         NR 823 M Pan American Clipper

TRANSPACIFIC SURVEY FLIGHT 1935
NUMBER 2

San Francisco—Honolulu—Midway

Lv. San Francisco (Alameda) . . . 5:45 p.m. EST, June 12
Ar. Honolulu (Pearl Harbor) . . 11:42 a.m. EST, June 13

18 hrs.

Lv. Honolulu . . . . 5:57 a.m. HLT, June 15
Ar. Midway . . . . 3:10 p.m. HLT, June 15

9 hrs., 13 mins.

Lv. Midway . . . . 6:00 a.m. MDY, June 17
Ar. Honolulu . . . . 5:34 p.m. HNL, June 17

10 hrs., 6 mins.

Lv. Honolulu . . . . 3:30 p.m. HLT, June 21
Ar. San Francisco . . . . 12:40 p.m. PT, June 22

18 hrs., 40 mins.

CREW: Captain Edwin C. Musick
      1st Officer R.O.D. Sullivan
      Engineering Officer V.A. Wright
      Jr. Flight Officer H.R. Canaday
      Navigation Officer F.J. Noonan
      Radio Officer W.T. Jarboe, Jr.

AIRCRAFT: Sikorsky S-42
         NR 823 M Pan American Clipper

TRANSPACIFIC SURVEY FLIGHT 1935
NUMBER 3

San Francisco—Honolulu—Midway—Wake

Lv. San Francisco (Alameda) . . . . August 9
Ar. Honolulu (Pearl Harbor) . . . . August 10

17 hrs., 12 mins.

Lv. Honolulu . . . . A.M., August 13
Ar. Midway . . . . P.M., August 13

8 hrs., 50 mins.

Lv. Midway . . . . A.M., August 16
International Dateline (+) Day
Ar. Wake . . . . P.M., August 17

8 hrs., 9 mins.

Lv. Wake . . . . A.M., August 21
International Dateline (–) Day
Ar. Midway . . . . P.M., August 20

8 hrs., 44 mins.

Lv. Midway . . . . A.M., August 22
Ar. Honolulu . . . . P.M., August 22

10 hrs., 7 mins.

Lv. Honolulu . . . . August 27
Ar. San Francisco . . . . 10:55 a.m., August 28

17 hrs., 25 mins.

CREW: Captain R.O.D. Sullivan
      1st Officer J.H. Tilton
      Engineering Officer V.A. Wright
      2nd Engineering Officer P. Berst
      Jr. Flight Officer H.R. Canaday
      Jr. Flight Officer M. Weber
      Navigation Officer F.J. Noonan
      Radio Officer W.T. Jarboe, Jr.

AIRCRAFT: Sikorsky S-42
         NR 823 M Pan American Clipper

TRANSPACIFIC SURVEY FLIGHT 1935
NUMBER 4

San Francisco—Honolulu—Midway—Wake—Guam

Lv. San Francisco (Alameda) . 3:00 p.m. PST, October 5
Ar. Honolulu (Pearl Harbor) . 3:05 a.m. PST, October 6

17 hrs., 22 mins.

Lv. Honolulu . . . . A.M., October 10
Ar. Midway . . . . P.M., October 10

9 hrs., 13 mins.

Lv. Midway . . . . A.M., October 11
International Dateline (+) Day
Ar. Wake . . . . P.M., October 12

9 hrs., 37 mins.

Lv. Wake . . . . A.M., October 13
Ar. Guam . . . . P.M., October 13

10 hrs., 27 mins.

Lv. Guam . . . . A.M., October 16
Ar. Wake . . . . P.M., October 16

12 hrs., 4 mins.

Lv. Wake . . . . A.M., October 17
International Dateline (–) Day
Ar. Midway . . . . P.M., October 16

9 hrs., 49 mins.

Lv. Midway . . . . A.M., October 19
Ar. Honolulu . . . . P.M., October 19

9 hrs., 49 mins.

Lv. Honolulu . . . . P.M., October 23
Ar. San Francisco . . . . P.M., October 24

17 hrs., 42 mins.

CREW: Captain R.O.D. Sullivan
1st Officer J.H. Tilton
2nd Officer M. Lodeesen
Engineering Officer V.A. Wright
Jr. Flight Officer H.R. Canaday
Navigation Officer F.J. Noonan
Radio Officer W.T. Jarboe, Jr.

AIRCRAFT: Sikorsky S-42
NR 823 M Pan American Clipper

TIME: San Francisco—Guam: 46 hrs., 39 mins.
Guam—San Francisco: 48 hrs., 45 mins.
Total: 95 hrs., 24 mins.

FIRST TRANSPACIFIC PASSENGER FLIGHT
October 21-27, 1936

Hawaii Clipper NC14714 Martin M-130
San Francisco, California—Manila, Philippine Islands

Passengers from San Francisco to Manila:

R.F. Bradley (Ticket #1)
Aviation manager, Standard Oil, San Francisco
office

Wilbur May
Los Angeles department store executive

T.F. Ryan III
San Francisco capitalist

Col. Charles Bartley
Chicago—large grocery firm

* Alfred Bennett
Hightstown, N.J.
Aviation executive

Mrs. Clara Adams
Stroudsburg, Penn.
World traveller—"First Flighter"

Mrs. Zetta Averill
Aberdeen, Wash.
World traveller

Mr. Bennett debarked at Honolulu.

Passengers from Honolulu to Manila:

Dr. Hilario Moncado
G.R. Carter
Louis Weinzheimer
Edward Brier
Herbert Shipman

Crew:
Captain Edwin C. Musick
First Officer: H.E. Gray
Second Officer: Max Weber (Navigator)
Third Officer: E.C. Bierer (Junior Flight Officer)
Fourth Officer: Chauncey Wright
(Engineering Officer)
Fifth Officer: T.R. Runnells (Radio Officer)
Sixth Officer: Frederick Noonan
(Navigation Instructor)
Steward: L.R. Merrill

Aircraft departed Alameda Base, San Francisco,
California, on Oct. 21, 1936 and arrived at Cavite
Base, Manila, Philippine Islands, on Oct. 27, 1936.

PAN AMERICAN AIRWAYS, INC. CAB DOCKET NO. 851 et al

History of Schedules, Frequencies and Changes in Equipment on Transpacific Services—North Pacific

DATE	ROUTING	TYPE OF EQUIPMENT	FREQUENCY	ELAPSED TIME	REMARKS
Nov. 22, 1935 to May 10, 1936	San Francisco—Honolulu—Midway—Wake—Guam—Manila.	M-130	2 per month	5 Days; 10:00 (approx.)	San Francisco departures scheduled, with U.S. Post Office authorization, as follows: Nov. 22; Dec. 6; Dec. 20, 1935; Jan. 3; Feb. 9; Feb. 19; March 15; March 29; April 13; April 30, 1936.
May 10, 1936 to July 8, 1936	San Francisco—Honolulu—Midway—Wake—Guam—Manila	M-130	3 per month	5 Days; 10:00 (approx.)	San Francisco departures scheduled, with U.S. Post Office authorization, as follows: May 10; May 20; May 31; June 10; June 20; June 30, 1936.
July 8, 1936 to Dec. 1, 1937	San Francisco—Honolulu—Midway—Wake—Guam—Manila	M-130	Weekly	5 Days; 10:00 (approx.)	Scheduled to depart San Francisco on Wednesdays.
April 28, 1937 to Dec. 1, 1937	Manila—Macau—Hong Kong	S-42	Weekly	6:15	Eastbound, Manila-Hong Kong direct. Connect with San Francisco-Manila service.
Dec. 1, 1937 to Aug. 6, 1938	San Francisco—Honolulu—Midway—Wake—Guam—Manila—Macau—Hong Kong	M-130	Weekly	6 Days; 8:30	Eastbound, Manila-Hong Kong direct.
Aug. 6, 1938 to Feb. 22, 1939	San Francisco—Honolulu—Midway—Wake—Guam—Manila—Macau—Hong Kong	M-130	3 per month (approx.)	6 Days; 8:35	Weekly service impracticable due to loss of NC 14714. San Francisco departures scheduled, with U.S. Post Office authorization, as follows: Aug. 6; Aug. 17; Aug. 24; Aug. 31; Sept. 7; Sept. 14; Sept. 21; Oct. 5; Oct. 12; Oct. 26; Nov. 2; Nov. 16; Nov. 23; Dec. 7; Dec. 14; Dec. 28, 1938; Jan. 14; Jan. 21; Feb. 1; Feb. 15, 1939.
Feb. 22, 1939 to May 2, 1941	San Francisco—Honolulu—Midway—Wake—Guam—Manila—Macau—Hong Kong	M-130; B-314	Weekly	6 Days; 7:20	Increase in schedule made possible by acquisition of NC 18602, Jan. 28, 1939; and NC 18601, March 2, 1939. Depart San Francisco Wednesdays until Oct. 30, 1939; thereafter Tuesdays.
May 2, 1941 to Sept. 30, 1941	San Francisco—Honolulu—Midway—Wake—Guam—Manila—Macau—Hong Kong	M-130; B-314	Bi-weekly	6 Days; 7:20	Alternate weeks to Singapore.
May 2, 1941 to Sept. 30, 1941	San Francisco—Honolulu—Midway—Wake—Guam—Manila—Singapore	M-130; B-314	Bi-weekly	6 Days; 9:35	Alternate weeks to Hong Kong.

DATE	ROUTING	TYPE OF EQUIPMENT	FREQUENCY	ELAPSED TIME	REMARKS
Aug. 7, 1941 to Sept. 30, 1941	San Francisco—Honolulu	M-130; B-314	Bi-weekly	19:45	
Sept. 30, 1941	San Francisco—Honolulu	M-130; B-314	Bi-weekly	17:45	
Sept. 30, 1941	Manila—Macau—Hong Kong	S-42	2 per week	6:40	
Sept. 30, 1941	San Francisco—Honolulu—Midway—Guam—Manila—Singapore	M-130; B-314	Weekly	6 Days; 9:05	Reduction in elapsed time per published schedule effective Sept. 30, 1941. Eastbound, Manila-Hong Kong direct. Connect with San Francisco-Singapore service at Manila.

All stations except Macau were overnight. Aircraft departed California in the afternoon, arrived Honolulu the next morning, and departed Honolulu—Midway the following morning.

History of Schedules, Frequencies and Changes in Equipment on Transpacific Services—South Pacific

DATE	ROUTING	TYPE OF EQUIPMENT	FREQUENCY	ELAPSED TIME	REMARKS
July 12, 1940 to Aug. 7, 1941	San Francisco—Los Angeles—Honolulu—Canton—Noumea—Auckland	B-314	Bi-weekly	4 Days; 9:00	
Aug. 7, 1941 to Oct. 30, 1941	San Francisco—Los Angeles—Honolulu—Canton—Noumea—Auckland	M-130; B-314	Bi-weekly	4 Days; 7:45	Although the current schedule provided for this route to be flown by M-130s and B-314s, only B-314 equipment was used.
Aug. 7, 1941	San Francisco—Los Angeles—Honolulu	M-130; B-314	Bi-weekly	23:00	
Aug. 7, 1941	Los Angeles—Honolulu	M-130; B-314	Bi-weekly	19:00	
Oct. 30, 1941	San Francisco—Los Angeles—Honolulu—Canton—Suva—Noumea—Auckland	M-130; B-314	Bi-weekly	5 Days; 7:50	

All stations except Los Angeles were overnight. Aircraft departed California in the afternoon, arrived Honolulu the next morning, and departed Honolulu—Canton the following morning.

FIRST TRANSPACIFIC AIRMAIL FLIGHT
LOG OF THE CHINA CLIPPER
1935

WEST BOUND

L. San Francisco	3:46 p.m., Friday, Nov. 22
A. Honolulu	10:19 a.m., Saturday, Nov. 23
L. Honolulu	6:35 a.m., Sunday, Nov. 24
A. Midway	2:00 p.m., Sunday, Nov. 24
L. Midway	6:12 a.m., Monday, Nov. 25

Time advanced one day crossing
International Dateline westbound

A. Wake	1:38 p.m., Tuesday, Nov. 26
L. Wake	6:01 a.m., Wednesday, Nov. 27
A. Guam	3:05 p.m., Wednesday, Nov. 27

Remained one day according original
schedule to arrive Manila November 29

L. Guam	6:12 a.m., Friday, Nov. 29
A. Manila	3:32 p.m., Friday, Nov. 29

Local Times Throughout
Westbound: 8,210 miles—59 hrs., 48 mins.

EAST BOUND

L. Manila	2:53 a.m., Monday, Dec. 2
A. Guam	6:41 p.m., Monday, Dec. 2
L. Guam	6:11 a.m., Tuesday, Dec. 3
A. Wake	8:57 p.m., Tuesday, Dec. 3
L. Wake	6:45 a.m., Wednesay, Dec. 4

Time retarded one day crossing
International Dateline eastbound

A. Midway	4:49 p.m., Tuesday, Dec. 3
L. Midway	6:11 a.m., Wednesday, Dec. 4
A. Hawaii	3:02 p.m., Wednesday, Dec. 4
L. Hawaii	3:02 p.m., Thursday, Dec. 5
A. San Francisco	10:36 a.m., Friday, Dec. 6

Local Times Throughout

Eastbound: 8,210 miles—63 hrs., 24 mins.
Total Flight: 16,420 miles—123 hrs., 12 mins.

LOG OF FIRST TRANSPACIFIC PASSENGER FLIGHT
SAN FRANCISCO—MANILA
1936

WEST BOUND

L. San Francisco (Alameda)	Wednesday, Oct. 21
A. Honolulu (Pearl Harbor)	Thursday, Oct. 22
L. Honolulu	Friday, Oct. 23
A. Midway	Friday, Oct. 23
L. Midway	Saturday, Oct. 24

Time advanced one day crossing
International Dateline westbound

A. Wake	Sunday, Oct. 25
L. Wake	Monday, Oct. 26
A. Guam	Monday, Oct. 26
L. Guam	Tuesday, Oct. 27
A. Manila (Cavite)	Tuesday, Oct. 27

Westbound: 7,309 miles
56 hrs., 22 mins. flying time

EAST BOUND

L. Manila (Cavite)	Saturday, Oct. 31
A. Guam	Saturday, Oct. 31
L. Guam	Sunday, Nov. 1
A. Wake	Sunday, Nov. 1
L. Wake	Monday, Nov. 2

Time retarded one day crossing
International Dateline eastbound

A. Midway	Monday, Nov. 2
L. Midway	Monday, Nov. 2
A. Honolulu	Tuesday, Nov. 3
L. Honolulu (Pearl Harbor)	Tuesday, Nov. 3
A. San Francisco (Alameda)	Wednesday, Nov. 4

Eastbound: 7,056 miles
63 hrs., 13 mins. flying time

7 Passengers SFO-HNL   Martin M-130 Flying Boat   10 Passengers MNL-HNL
11 Passengers HNL-MNL   Hawaii Clipper NC 14714   8 Passengers HNL-SFO

SHANGHAI-PEIPING LINE

					Round trip
Shanghai	45	95	160	240	270
25	Nanking	50	120	210	250
55	30	Haichow	70	180	200
90	70	40	Tsingtao	120	140
130	120	100	70	Tientsin	45
150	140	110	80	25	Peiping

Single trip.

SHANGHAI-CANTON LINE

					Round trip
Shanghai	115	205	270	300	390
65	Wenchow	100	180	230	340
115	55	Foochow	80	140	270
150	100	45	Amoy	60	195
170	130	80	35	Swatow	135
220	190	150	110	75	Canton

Single trip.
All above fares in dollars of Chinese national currency.
For passenger baggage allowance, 15 kilos free.

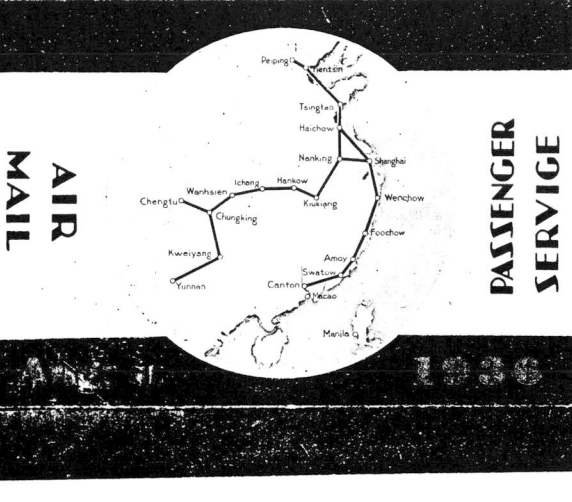

CNAC schedule, August 1936.

TIME TABLES

SHANGHAI-CHENGTU LINE

West bound — East bound

Express M. We. Fr. (Douglas)	Tu. Thur. Sat. Sun. (Douglas)	Read Down		Read Up	Mon. Wed. Fri. Sun. (Douglas)	Express Tu. Th. Sa. (Douglas)
7.00	7.00	Lv.	Shanghai	Ar.	*10.55	*17.30
8.20	8.20	Lv.	Nanking	Lv.	*9.40	*16.15
10.00	10.00	Lv.	Kiukiang	Lv.	8.00	14.35
10.55*	10.55* (Loening)	Ar.	Hankow	Lv.	7.00 (Loening)	13.35
11.20*	7.30	Lv.	Hankow	Ar.	15.40	13.10
	9.10	Lv.	Shasi	Lv.	14.15	
12.35*	10.10	Lv.	Ichang	Lv.	13.15	12.00
	12.30	Lv.	Wanhsien	Lv.	10.55	
14.35*	14.10 (Stinson)	Ar.	Chungking	Lv.	9.00 (Stinson)	9.55
15.00*	14.30	Lv.	Chungking	Ar.	14.00	9.30
16.15*	16.30	Ar.	Chengtu	Lv.	12.00	8.15

*Note: In case the plane flies direct from Nanking to Hankow or Hankow to Nanking, the remainder of schedule will be advanced by 40 minutes.

SHANGHAI-PEIPING LINE

North bound — South bound

Express M. We. Sa. (Douglas)	Tu. Th. Fri. Sun. (Stinson)	Read Down		Read Up	Tu. Th. Fri. Sun. (Stinson)	Express M. We. Sa. (Douglas)
6.00	6.30	Lv.	Shanghai	Ar.	14.45	18.55
7.20		Lv.	Nanking	Lv.		17.40
	9.30	Lv.	Haichow	Lv.	12.00	
9.45	11.05	Lv.	Tsingtao	Lv.	10.25	15.35
11.35	14.05	Lv.	Tientsin	Lv.	7.25	13.25
12.10	14.45	Ar.	Peiping	Lv.	6.30	12.45

SHANGHAI-CANTON LINE

South bound — North bound

Tue. Thur. (Dolphin)	Read Down		Read Up	Thur. Sun. (Dolphin)
6.30	Lv.	Shanghai	Ar.	15.00
8.45	Lv.	Wenchow	Lv.	13.05
10.25	Lv.	Foochow	Lv.	11.25
11.55	Lv.	Amoy	Lv.	9.55
13.15	Lv.	Swatow	Lv.	8.35
15.00	Ar.	Canton	Lv.	6.30

PASSENGER FARE TABLES
SHANGHAI-CHENGTU LINE

								Round trip
S'hai	45	180	210	300	335	500	610	720
25	N'king	135	180	270	305	470	580	680
100	75	K'kiang	65	155	190	355	495	655
120	100	35	H'kow	90	125	290	430	590
170	150	85	50	Shasi	45	215	360	520
190	170	105	70	25	Ichang	180	325	485
280	260	195	160	120	100	W'hsien	155	315
340	320	275	240	200	180	85	C'king	160
400	380	365	330	290	270	175	90	Ch'tu

Single Trip.
All above fares in dollars of Chinese National Currency.
CHINA NATIONAL AVIATION CORPORATION
51 Canton Road, Shanghai — Telephone 12955

PAA

PAN AMERICAN CLIPPERS 1934–1945

PAN AM NUMBER	DATE DELIVERED	REMARKS
SIKORSKY S-42		
NC-822M	May 1934	Fate unknown
NC-823M	December 1934	Scrapped 1946
NC-824M	May 1935	Crashed, Cuba, 1944
NC-15373 (A)	July 1935	Crashed, Trinidad, 1935
NC-15374 (A)	December 1935	Scrapped 1946
NC-15375 (A)	February 1936	Scrapped 1946
NC-15376 (A)	April 1936	Scrapped 1946
NC-16734 (B)	September 1936	Crashed, Samoa, 1938
NC-16735 (B)	September 1936	Sunk, Hong Kong, 1941
NC-16736 (B)	1937	Burned, Manos, Brazil, 1943
MARTIN M-130		
NC-14714	March 1936	Crashed? Pacific 1938
Hawaii Clipper		
NC-14715	November 1935	Crashed, California, 1943
Philippine Clipper		
NC-14716	October 1935	Crashed, Trinidad, 1945
China Clipper		
BOEING B-314		
NC-18601	January 1939	Crashed, 1945
Honolulu Clipper		
NC-18602	January 1939	Fate unknown
California Clipper		
NC-18603	February 1939	Crashed, Lisbon, Portugal, 1943
Yankee Clipper		
NC-18604	March 1939	Fate unknown
Atlantic Clipper		
NC-18605	April 1939	Fate unknown
Dixie Clipper		
NC-18606	June 1939	Fate unknown
American Clipper		
NC-18607 (A)	April 1941	Sold to BOAC; became G-AGBZ "Bristol"
NC-18608 (A)	April 1941	Sold to BOAC; became G-AGCA "Berwick"
NC-18609 (A)	May 1941	Fate unknown
Pacific Clipper		
NC-18610 (A)	April 1941	Sold to BOAC; became G-AGCB "Bangor"
NC-18611 (A)	June 1941	Fate unknown
Anzac Clipper		
NC-18612 (A)	July 1941	Fate unknown
Capetown Clipper		

Data from M.D. Klaas courtesy of Richard Paul Symers.

*In 1948 the three B-314s owned by BOAC were sold to General Phoenix Corp. of New York.

AIRPLANE COMPARISONS*

	S-42	M-130	B-314
NUMBER BUILT	10 (Sikorsky)	3 (Martin)	12 (Boeing)
GROSS WEIGHT	38,000#	51,000#	82,500#
EMPTY WEIGHT	19,000#	28,000#	50,000#
WING SPAN	118' 2"	130'	152'
LENGTH	69'	90' 10"	106'
HEIGHT	21' 9"	24'	27' 7"
TOP SPEED	182 mph	180 mph	193 mph
CRUISING SPEED	140-145 mph	130 mph	150 mph
RANGE	1,200 miles	3,200 miles	3,000 miles
NO. OF ENGINES	4	4	4
HORSEPOWER (EACH)	750	800	1,500
CREW	4	5-7	7-10
PASSENGERS	28-32	36 (18 Night)	74 (36 Night)

*These figures changed with variations of each flying-boat.

Ceremony on Midway Island.   Alan Wright

A monument was dedicated at the Pearl City Clipper base site.   Alan Wright

On Nov. 22, 1985, Pan Am recreated the first Pacific airmail flight of 50 years before. This time a 747 was used. Each former clipper base was visited by the approximately 300 passengers. This gathering was taken on Wake Island.   PAA

Historian Neil Malloch of the California Heritage Council hurls a wreath into San Francisco Bay on March 27, 1985, to commemorate the sailing of the *North Haven* exactly 50 years ago. Also on hand on Pier 22 were Terry Hamid of the Port of San Francisco, Janet Davis of the Friends of the Port of San Francisco, Joseph Pease, former Pan Am employee and Oren Holmes.
Courtesy *San Francisco Chronicle*. Eric Luse photographer

BIBLIOGRAPHY

Bender, Marylin & Selig Altschul, *The Chosen Instrument, Juan Trippe, Pan Am, The Rise and Fall of an American Entrepreneur,* Simon & Schuster, New York, 1982.

Brock, Horace, *Flying the Oceans, A Pilot's Story of Pan Am,* The Stinehour Press, Lunenburg, Vt., 1978.

Daley, Robert, *An American Saga, Juan Trippe and His Pan Am Empire,* Random House, New York, 1980.

Davies, R.E.G., *Airlines of the United States Since 1914,* Putnam, London, 1972, Smithsonian Institution Press, 1983.

Day, Beth, *The Manila Hotel, The Heart and Memory of a City,* National Media Production Center, Manila.

Holmes, Donald B., *Air Mail, An Illustrated History, 1793-1981,* Clarkson N. Potter, New York, 1981.

Jablonski, Edward, *Sea Wings, The Romance of the Flying Boats,* Doubleday & Co., Garden City, N.Y., 1972.

Jackson, Ronald W., *China Clipper,* Everest House, New York, 1980.

Kaucher, Dorothy, *Wings Over Wake,* John Howell, San Francisco, Calif., 1947.

Miller, William Burke, "Flying the Pacific," *National Geographic,* December 1936, Vol. LXX, No. 6.

Turner, P. St. John, *Pictorial History of Pan American World Airways,* Ian Allan Ltd., London, 1973.

The author holding a piece of the *Philippine Clipper* which crashed in California in 1943. The piece was provided by Gordon Werne of Oakland, California.

ABOUT THE AUTHOR

Stan Cohen is a native of West Virginia and a 1961 graduate of West Virginia University with a BS degree in geology. After years spent running his own ski business, directing a historical park in Missoula, Montana, and acting as a consulting geologist, he launched Pictorial Histories Publishing Company in 1976.

To date he has authored or co-authored 55 books and published a total of 180, most of which deal with military-history subjects. His particular interest is the early Pacific campaigns of World War II. Mr. Cohen currently lived in Missoula with his wife, Anne. He enjoys traveling and skiing, and collects antique cars and early paper Americana.

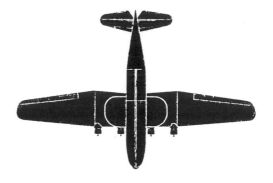